FORGOTTEN ROYAL WOMEN

THE KING AND I

FORGOTTEN ROYAL WOMEN

THE KING AND I

Woolavington
Village Hall
Exchange Library
Read Return Donate

ERIN LAWLESS

PEN & SWORD
HISTORY
AN IMPRINT OF PEN & SWORD BOOKS LTD.
YORKSHIRE – PHILADELPHIA

First published in Great Britain in 2019 by
PEN AND SWORD HISTORY
An imprint of
Pen & Sword Books Ltd
Yorkshire – Philadelphia

ISBN 978 1 47389 817 2

A CIP catalogue record for this book is available from the British Library.

Printed and bound in the UK by TJ International
Typeset in Times New Roman 11.5/14 by
Aura Technology and Software Services, India

Pen & Sword Books Limited incorporates the imprints of Atlas, Archaeology,
Aviation, Discovery, Family History, Fiction, History, Maritime, Military, Military
Classics, Politics, Select, Transport, True Crime, Air World, Frontline Publishing,
Leo Cooper, Remember When, Seaforth Publishing, The Praetorian Press,
Wharncliffe Local History, Wharncliffe Transport, Wharncliffe True Crime and
White Owl.

For a complete list of Pen & Sword titles please contact
PEN & SWORD BOOKS LIMITED
47 Church Street, Barnsley, South Yorkshire, S70 2AS, England
E-mail: enquiries@pen-and-sword.co.uk
Website: www.pen-and-sword.co.uk

Or
PEN AND SWORD BOOKS
1950 Lawrence Rd, Havertown, PA 19083, USA
E-mail: Uspen-and-sword@casematepublishers.com
Website: www.penandswordbooks.com

Contents

Introduction

Catherine, the heroine of Jane Austen's *Northanger Abbey*, bemoans studying history as boring, not least because 'the men [are] all so good for nothing, and [there are] hardly any women at all'. And she's not wrong, is she? British history, if you stand back, can seem just a chain of Edwards and Henrys and Georges, from royalty right down to the commoners. They enter stage left, and exit stage right, and there aren't really many ladies standing with them come the curtain call.

There are some women, of course. I asked people who came to mind when they thought of royal women and some big-ticket names appeared again and again. These are the ones we all learn about in school, the 'key-stage' Queens, unusually memorable probably because they did something terribly public and unfeminine, like rule in their own stead, or die tragically:

Eleanor of Aquitaine, imperious in her starchy wimple, striding across the Alps in her old age. Ever enigmatic, the dark-eyed Anne Boleyn, who Henry VIII tumbled monasteries to have, before tumbling her head from the block. Victoria, clad in black, dour and dumpy, the Widow of Windsor, acerbically announcing herself to be 'not amused'. The Lady Diana Spencer, the 'Peoples' Princess', the 'Queen of Hearts', a bride barely out of her teens at the wedding of the century, who you could barely see for all the puff and pearls, along with Kate and Meghan, her modern-day daughter in laws.

Interestingly, not one person named any women from before the Conquest. In the UK we have rather fallen into the habit of taking our history as starting from 1066. A rhyme taught to me in school in the nineties began, rather dismissively, 'William the First was the first of our kings/Not counting the Ethelreds, Egberts and things'. Of course, the world didn't begin once William the Bastard set one Norman toe on Pevensey soil.

Nor, of course, have we just had kings. The British Isles have had (arguably, as is everything) ten women considered (by at least some) to be Queen Regnant (and that's about fifteen per cent of the total, since the Conquest). A woman sits on the metaphorical and literal throne of the United Kingdom today, and has done so for over 65 years. Back in 2013, pleasingly aligned with but not a result of the birth of Prince William's baby daughter, changes to the laws of succession were ratified, meaning that future British princesses will not get bumped down the order when baby brothers are born. History books of the future will probably have much more fodder when it comes to the topic of British royal women (a Republican coup notwithstanding, naturally).

But this book isn't about Queen Regnants. It's not even just about Queen Consorts. Because yes, most kings had a wife (sometimes multiple wives), but they also had sisters, aunts, daughters and cousins, women we only hear about when their lives intersect with those of their menfolk. Huge swathes of their lives are unknown to us even now, and probably always will be. They worked their politics quietly in the bedroom, not the state room; they died privately in childbirth, not in battle. But that doesn't mean that there aren't stories there left to tell…

Scota

Scota is a pseudohistorical character in Irish and Scottish mythology, the daughter of an Egyptian Pharoah to whom the Gaels liked to trace their ancestry; she allegedly explains the name Scoti applied by the Romans to Irish raiders, and later to the Irish invaders of what would later be known as Scotland.

If Scota lived at all, she lived sometime in the centuries around 1400 BC. Tradition holds her as a daughter of either the Pharaoh Nectanebo or of Pharoah Akhenaten and his consort Nefertiti. According to the historian Eusebius, she was married to a Scythian prince. 'Scota' was probably an archetypal name bestowed upon her at this time; originally it was probably 'Sacathach' or 'Scythian', a title given to the foreign princess as a gesture of acceptance by her new husband's people. This Scythian prince is known by various names in the various sources but most commonly as Nel (later Latinised into 'Miles'), an individual who apparently assisted in the building of the Tower of Babel and was famed for being proficient in many languages. Nel was a younger twin, and since his brother was the accepted Scythian heir he was forced to travel to seek his fortune in Europe.

Eventually Nel and Scota stopped in Spain, where they there seemingly wasn't a terrible amount to do, as they soon had eight sons. Nel's beloved uncle was sent out as the head of an exploratory expedition to find somewhere that the ex-pat Scythians could settle permanently. When this uncle was captured, tortured and killed by the indigenous tribesmen of what would become Ireland, it became personal for Nel. He settled his people in Kerry on the south-western coast and took up arms against the tribesmen. They fought their way to Tara – the ancient capital city of the indigenous Irish and later the spot where the High Kings of Ireland were crowned – but Nel died the night before a decisive battle.

In true Egyptian queen style, Scota took control of her husband's men and led them in their final advance during the Battle of Tralee. Defeated, the indigenous tribesmen retreated into the hills but Scota – eager to claim a decisive victory – pursued them and was cut down. As seventeenth century poet Thomas Parnell immortalises:

> 'In yon cool glen, beside the mount, close by the wave, fell Scota while pursuing the enemy across the hills. Though Scota died early in the fray, her forces went on to victory and it is she that is remembered'.

Scota's grave reputedly lies in a valley, south of Tralee town, in an area known as Glenn Scoithin. A trail from the road leads along a stream to a clearing where a circle of large stones marks the grave site. No formal archaeology has ever been undertaken in this glen to establish the legend's validity either way.

Nel and Scota's eldest surviving son – Gaedheal – gave his name to the Gaelic people and language. The Gaels became overlords to the indigenous people of Ireland, and after a few generations, expanded over the Irish Sea to Scotland.

At his coronation in 1249, the Scottish King Alexander III heard his royal genealogy recited back through 56 generations back to Scota. It was also accepted that the Stone of Destiny – the flat rock upon which all Kings of Scotland (and thereafter Britain) were crowned – had been brought over from Egypt by Scota herself. The Scottish Declaration of Independence (Declaration of Arbroath, 1320 A.D.) makes the following statement:

> 'We know, Most Holy Father and Lord, and from the chronicles and books of the ancients gather, that among other illustrious nations, ours, to wit THE NATION OF THE SCOTS, has been distinguished by many honours; which PASSING FROM THE GREATER SCYTHIA through the Mediterranean Sea and Pillars of Hercules, and SOJOURNING IN SPAIN among the most savage tribes through a long course of time, could nowhere be subjugated by any people however barbarous AND COMING THENCE ONE THOUSAND TWO HUNDRED YEARS AFTER THE OUTGOING OF THE PEOPLE OF ISRAEL,

> THEY, BY MANY VICTORIES AND INFINITE TOIL, ACQUIRED FOR THEMSELVES THE POSSESSIONS IN THE WEST, WHICH THEY NOW HOLD…'

It might sound like just another flighty origin myth, but it is certainly true that the Gaels had come to Ireland by the Late Bronze Age. Some of the dates and names in the legend do accord with parts of the accepted history of both Ireland and Egypt. The wrecks of two Egyptian ships, discovered near Hull in 1937, have been radio-carbon-dated to the period 1400–1350 BC.

In 1955, archaeologists were excavating an ancient burial mound in Tara and discovered the skeleton of a Bronze Age prince, carbon dated once again to around 1400–1350 BC, wearing a rare Egyptian necklace of faience beads. Stones inlaid in the golden collar found around the neck of the boy-Pharaoh Tutankhamen are of identical manufacture and design… so maybe it's not such a leap of faith to imagine an Egyptian Warrior Queen riding wildly through the hills of Tralee.

Cartimandua

Cartimandua (ruled c.43–69) was a queen of the Brigantes, a Celtic people in what is now Yorkshire.

A contemporary of the rebellious – and much more famous – Boudica, she is the only queen that the Romans recognised in her own right, referring to her as 'regina' in their writings. Her name may be a compound of common Celtic roots, meaning either 'well-groomed' or 'sleek' pony (mandu). There is very little archaeological evidence of fortified hillforts in the north of Britain, as opposed to the south, and this is taken as a sign of peace and stability throughout her lands.

Cartimandua was already queen of the Brigantes when the Roman Emperor Claudius began his organised conquest of Britannia in 43. It is not made clear as to whether or not she was a puppet placed there by Rome or had ruled prior to their arrival. What is clear, however, was that she was royal-born. She was ruling as queen in her own right and the kingship of the Brigantes only came with marriage to her. It could be that she was the daughter and legitimate heir of the previous king, making installation by the Romans seem less likely. Her husband and king-consort was one Venutius, also of royal stock, but perhaps from a lesser bloodline.

Either way, when the Romans arrived in 43, the Brigantes were one of eleven tribes of Britannia who surrendered to Claudius. From this point on, Cartimandua was a 'client-queen' of Rome. Another tribe who capitulated at this time were the Iceni, ruled by Prasutagus, husband of Boudica. It seems that the Celts were well aware that they could not hope to succeed in the face of Roman imperialist might and were perhaps compromising with 'joint rule' in order to maintain as much of their culture and freedoms as possible.

Not all the indigenous tribes surrendered. The Catuvellauni king, Caratacus, became the de facto resistance leader of the rebellious Brits.

In 51, he was defeated by the Romans in Wales and sought sanctuary in Brigante land. Cartimandua, mindful of her arrangement with the Romans, felt she had no choice but to hand Caratacus over to them in chains, effectively breaking the back of the Celtic resistance.

This act of betrayal turned her husband Venutius' stomach. He separated from his wife and tried to take the kingdom by force. The Romans came to Cartimandua's aid, and Venutius – and those loyal to him – fled into exile. What had perhaps tipped Venutius over the edge was the fact that Cartimandua had taken another husband – this one, it appears, for love. He had once been Venutius' armour-bearer, and the two had been as close as brothers. His name was Vellocatus, meaning 'better in battle' (clearly better in some other respects too…). Although there were some grumbles about the unsuitability and low-birth of the new king-consort, Cartimandua remained queen – in collaboration with Rome – for a further nineteen years after her ex-husband's aborted rebellion. When Boudica took queenship of the Iceni after the death of her husband and raised her rebellion against Rome, Cartimandua did not send Brigante forces to aid either side, skilfully keeping her people neutral and safe.

By 69, Rome was suffering from internal political strife; it was known as the 'year of four Emperors'. The long-exiled Venutius saw his chance and invaded. As he had probably foreseen, the Romans were in no position to expend time and resources on such a small concern as the Brigantes. Venutius' coup was successful; Vellocatus was slain and Cartimandua fled the north of England, and was lost into the mists of history. Nobody knows where she lived out her days, or where she is buried. Rome eventually annexed the Brigante land completely.

What makes Cartimandua so interesting is that the Romans treated with her at all. Although Celtic society was very modern in respect to their allowing women to rule and fight alongside their men, the Roman world was very traditional. Women had their place and that place was not one of power or control. Cartimandua went directly against Roman societal norms, yet unlike Boudica and her daughters, she was allowed to keep her position. She led a stable and peaceful realm for twenty years, whilst the rest of the British Isles were falling under a Roman tyranny. Boudica is remembered for being brave enough to fight the imperialist invaders, but Cartimandua – when she is remembered at all – is derided for being a coward and an adulteress with her husband's servant. She should perhaps be remembered for a different kind of bravery, that of facing the diplomacy and capitulation necessary to keep her people safe and prosperous.

Perhaps the most enduring legacy that this early queen has left us is the Arthurian legend, which would come to prominence centuries later. Some scholars believe that the true life Cartimandua/Venutius/Vellocatus love triangle was the basis for the story of Gwenhwyfar/Guinevere – Arthur's queen – and her affair with his companion, Lancelot, that lead to the downfall of Camelot. Although we of course can never know for sure, the parallels between the tales are thought-provoking indeed.

Judith of Flanders

Judith of Flanders (c.843–870) was a great-granddaughter of Charlemagne, the eldest daughter of the Frankish King and Holy Roman Emperor, Charles the Bald of the House of the Carolingians. She was twice-over Queen of Wessex, the dominant and largest Anglo-Saxon kingdom.

In 855 King Æthelwulf of Wessex, an extremely pious man, made a pilgrimage to Rome. On his way back the following year, he took rest at the court of the Holy Roman Emperor. Both men, it seems, were growing increasingly troubled by the aggression of the Vikings and were interested in making an alliance.

Æthelwulf had a handfast wife, a Saxon woman called Osburh who had given him a daughter and five sons – four of whom would eventually rule as King of Wessex. Perhaps she had died by the time of Æthelwulf's pilgrimage, or perhaps – like so many other Saxon handfast wives – she was put aside, as Æthelwulf agreed to marry the Emperor Charles' firstborn daughter. Æthelwulf was approaching 60, whilst this girl – Judith – would have been around 13. Charles insisted that his daughter be treated with the utmost respect, and be formally crowned and known as Queen, which was not customary in Saxon England at the time.

Whilst it is clear that this union was for diplomatic purposes and not for the getting of further heirs, the marriage provoked a rebellion by Æthelwulf's eldest surviving son, Æthelbald, who feared displacement in the line of succession by a higher born half-brother. However, father and son soon negotiated a compromise, where Æthelbald was reaffirmed as his father's heir and given the sub-kingship of Kent.

As it turned out, Æthelbald had no need for concern, as Judith never had children by Æthelwulf, who died on 13 January 858. He was succeeded, as promised, by Æthelbald as his eldest surviving son. Judith, a Dowager Queen still only in her mid-teens, began making arrangements to return to the home of her father. Æthelbald moved quickly, marrying her, tying her and her Carolingian prestige once again to the House of Wessex.

All of Europe was aghast. The incest implicit in marrying your father's widow not only went against Christian law, but pagan sensibilities also. Realising the level of disgust he had inspired in his men, Æthelbald finally agreed to an annulment of the marriage on the grounds of consanguinity. It proved not to matter; he died before the year was out, to be succeeded by the next brother in line.

Having learnt her lesson, Judith moved even faster this time, liquidising her assets in Wessex and returning to her father, who promptly stuck her – for safekeeping, we assume – in a monastery. Over Christmas 861, with the collusion of her brother (the intriguingly named 'Louis the Stammerer') Judith eloped from the monastery with the man she had fallen in love with, Count Baldwin, and the pair fled north.

Emperor Charles was furious and immediately sent men after the couple. They managed to evade capture for almost a full year, before – in October 862 – they sought refuge at the court of Judith's cousin, Lothair II (of a now defunct kingdom west of the Rhine). Unable now to touch Judith and Baldwin, Charles attempted instead to damn their eternal souls, ordering his bishops to excommunicate them. Judith and Baldwin travelled onwards to Rome, where they had the Pope himself confirm the validity of their marriage. Charles now had no choice but to recognise the marital contract and he settled the area of Flanders upon his new son-in-law. Flanders would grow to become one of the most powerful principalities of France.

Judith gave Baldwin three sons, including the future Baldwin II, before dying young – even by the standards of the ninth century – in just her mid-twenties. Whilst her two royal marriages with the House of Wessex produced no children, she is – through her sons with Baldwin – the ancestress of Matilda of Flanders, the queen-consort of William the Conqueror, and therefore a genetic matriarch of the later monarchs of unified England.

Æthelflæd

Æthelflæd (868–918) was the eldest daughter of the beloved Saxon King Alfred the Great and was chronicled in the historical record as *Myrcna hlæfdige*, or 'Lady of the Mercians'.

Born to Alfred, King of Wessex and his queen, Ealhswith of the House of Mercia, Æthelflæd (meaning 'noble beauty') knew only strife and warfare. The Danes (or Vikings, if you prefer) had been harrying the Saxon shores in an attempt at conquest for generations, but during the reign of Alfred their ferocity had increased under the leadership of a warrior called Guthrum. Alfred could not stand against them and took to paying them a tithe in order that they stay out of Wessex. Although ostensibly there was peace, Guthrum attacked the royal household at Chippenham at Christmas 878. Alfred and his young family had to flee on foot through the woods, struggling to make it to a stronghold island fortress in the Somerset marshes, known as Athelney.

Here Alfred came up with a bold plan, a vision for the future that the young Æthelflæd absorbed at her father's knee. Alfred knew that to be strong, the Anglo-Saxons also had to be united – metaphysically as well as physically – under the same religion (namely Christianity) and adhering to the same canon of law. The crumbling Roman fortifications needed to be rebuilt and there needed to be a system where they could be manned year-round without neglecting the harvest, which so often happened in wartime, and lead to famine. As other kingdoms fell under Danish rule, still Wessex remained defiant, and the Saxon ealdormen began to flock to Alfred's banner and make his vision of a united country their own.

Alfred eventually triumphed over Guthrum, but it was a hard-won peace. Although Guthrum converted to Christianity and vowed not to enter Wessex again, Alfred had to give up swathes of Anglo-Saxon territory, mainly East Anglia and the eastern half of Mercia, to create a new Danish kingdom (hereafter known as the Danelaw). The territory also included the Mercian city of London. Alfred's capital was in Winchester, which is where Æthelflæd grew into her teens during this short period of uneasy peace.

It was likely that Alfred knew all along that it was only to be a short peace. For the six years afforded to him he worked to codify the laws of the country, formed a fine navy, rebuilt towns and cities that the Danes had once sacked, and created a clear administrative system to control taxation and promote trade. He began to style himself as 'King of the Anglo-Saxons' as opposed to merely King of Wessex.

The Ealdorman of Mercia was Æthelred, who hated the Danes even more than most for the destruction they had wrought on his kingdom. He travelled to the court at Winchester to learn more about Alfred's intentions for fortifying the Saxon kingdoms and there became impressed with the pre-teen princess, every inch her impressive father's daughter, who spoke to him knowledgeably about defying the Danes.

Æthelred returned to Mercia and wrested control of most of the western half back from the Danes. In 884, he sent for Æthelflæd, now around sixteen, with the promise to not only make her his consort, but his co-ruler in Mercia, an almost unprecedented position for a woman, even the daughter of the great Alfred. Alfred himself was thrilled, seeing the union of Wessex and Mercia through marriage as another step towards his dream of a fully unified 'Britannia'.

Alfred wasn't the only one to recognise the importance of this alliance. As Æthelflæd and her party made their way to Mercia for the marriage, the Danes attacked. Cool as anything, Æthelflæd commandeered a nearby ditch and used it as a military trench, defeating the enemy. In triumph she arrived at her new kingdom and was married.

Wessex and Mercia – or Æthelflæd and Æthelred – proved to be a dream team. In 885, a fresh band of Vikings appeared in Kent. The duplicitous Guthrum came to their aid and a furious Alfred joined together with his daughter and son-in-law to put Guthrum down. When they did, London and its territories was returned to the kingdom of Mercia. The uneasy peace with Guthrum and the Danelaw resumed.

Æthelflæd knew well what to do with the gift of a period of peace. Like her father before her she focused on securing and fostering trade and security, moving from one city to the next, rebuilding and fortifying, making Mercia a power to be wary of. In 888, she gave birth to her only child, a daughter, Ælfwynn, a difficult birth that left Æthelflæd unable to conceive again. Ælfwynn was doted upon, kept close to her mother and brought up to be a military leader. Æthelflæd was given wardship of her brother's son and heir, Æthelstan – the future king – and Ælfwynn was favoured with the same treatment and education as her illustrious cousin. Ælfwynn, however, never left her mother's side to marry, and some historians assume this was because Æthelflæd's long-term plan was for Mercia to be assimilated into Wessex, and so did not want for there to be a 'Mercian' heir.

Æthelflæd and Æthelred continued to wage battle against the Danes, focusing on the midlands and into the north, whilst Alfred and his heir – Æthelflæd's brother Edward – did the same in the south. Alfred died in 899, and Edward continued the fight. Having grown up closely with his sister, theirs was a natural alliance, and one that Æthelflæd needed more than ever, as in 902 her husband Æthelred was struck down by a strange, wasting disease. He was bed-ridden for the rest of his life, useless as a ruler, especially in this time of war.

Vikings chased out of Ireland attempted to settle in Chester, but they did not do so peacefully. Æthelflæd led her army to Chester, where she barricaded the city against the Danes, orchestrating a defence that involved large stones being dropped from the battlements. The canny Danes of course just approached the walls with shields held defensively above their heads. Æthelflæd's answer to this was to drop beehives instead, coating the Danes and their shields with sticky honey and the associated colonies of furious bees. Chester was saved and continued to prosper.

By the time Æthelred succumbed to his strange illness in 911, Æthelflæd had long been considered to be the ruler of Mercia in all but name. After she became widowed, she took on the portmanteau Lady of the Mercians, as opposed to Queen, wary not to offend any sensibilities and jeopardise her already socially precarious position. Regardless of semantics, Æthelflæd was highly respected and beloved. She was respected even by the Danes; chroniclers record how many Vikings surrendered to her without a fight. She proved herself not only a skilled military leader, but also a talented tactician. The *Annals of Ulster*, for example, state that her military success was 'through her own cleverness'.

In 917 it finally seemed as if the matter of the Danes in Britannia would finally be decided. Æthelflæd, along with an alliance of kings (Anglo-Saxon, Welsh and Scottish, showing that even the Celts and

Picts respected her) attacked the Danes in the city of Derby. It was a resounding victory, one so complete that the Danes of Leicester and York (great Viking strongholds) had absolutely no choice but to surrender.

With dreadful timing, Æthelflæd died only days before the Danes would have surrendered York to her, recognising her as their overlord. No record remains to tell us what the lady died of.. Perhaps it was of battle wound – she was around fifty when she died and her lifestyle had no doubt been a physically taxing one. She was mourned throughout the land and by all its people, even the Danes, who recognised her as a more than worthy adversary. She was buried in Gloucester, a city she had reconstructed from its Roman ruins, and laid out the core street plan, which is still that in existence today. She was succeeded as 'Lady of the Mercians' by her daughter, Ælfwynn, until her brother Edward came to assimilate Mercia into Wessex. It is likely that Ælfwynn lived out the rest of her life in a convent.

Æthelflæd was remembered as the 'perfect' leader; a formidable warrior, tempered by her gender to be kind and fair, brought up by her famous father to be intelligent and forward thinking. For all that she was careful to never be known as 'queen' in her lifetime, she comes down to us in history as exactly that. In the words of the *Annals of Ulster*, she was *Famosissima Regina Saxonium*, the 'most famous Queen of the Saxons'.

Ælfthryth

Ælfthryth (c.945–c.1001) was a Saxon Queen; wife, stepmother and mother to a succession of kings. She was the first king's wife known to have been crowned and anointed as Queen of the Kingdom of England.

Ælfthryth could be considered somewhat the original wicked stepmother. Nevertheless, she was a queen-regent of England, whose actions shaped the country (and the monarchy) we have today. Royal on both sides of her family, Ælfthryth's father was the Ealdorman of what is now Devon and her mother was of the royal family of Wessex. She was rumoured to be surpassingly lovely and Edgar, the king (known as 'the Peaceable') needed alliances in that part of his kingdom. He sent a trusted companion to scope her out as a potential bride. So lovely indeed was the young Ælfthryth that this companion married her himself, reporting back to Edgar that the girl was a hag.

His suspicions probably aroused, Edgar said he would meet with this girl himself and look upon her unfortunate face. Alarmed, the duplicitous companion ordered Ælfthryth to make herself look as ugly as possible for the king's visit. Showing the personality that would eventually have her known as a quarrelsome termagant, Ælfthryth did just the opposite. Edgar fell madly in love with her and his erstwhile friend soon found himself killed in a hunting 'accident'.

By all accounts, Ælfthryth was an effective queen and managed her vast estates and dower lands well. People petitioned her on a regular basis, suggesting she had the ear of the king and was allowed, at least in some capacity, to offer opinions and advice to him. She was extremely active in the matter of religious reform, supporting and renovating abbeys and other religious buildings.

Edgar had a bevy of children by his first two wives and Ælfthryth soon added two more sons to the total – the first was to die young, the second to become the derided Æthelred 'the Unready'. King Æthelred comes down to us through history as a weak and ineffectual king, forever remembered as 'unready' although the nickname, 'unraed', means more that he was ill-advised by his counsel rather than being particularly poorly prepared – and is particularly biting when you consider that ethelred actually means something like nobly counselled.

When Edgar died in 975, his son Edward (by his first wife), was almost grown; Æthelred could have been no older than nine or ten. By some accounts, Edward was not a likeable man and this may be the reason that the clergy and noblemen divided in loyalty between he and his half-brother Æthelred. Even after Edward was formally crowned King, the tension continued. Æthelred's supporters claimed that Edgar's first marriages had not been Christian ones, the wives never known as queens, and therefore all offspring from said marriages – Edward included – should be considered illegitimate and therefore unsuitable to rule.

In 978, King Edward came to Corfe Castle to visit his stepmother and half-brother. As he came through the gate, he was rushed by a clutch of men who pulled him from his horse and stabbed him to death in the castle courtyard. The previously unpopular Edward immediately and forevermore became known as 'Edward the Martyr'.

Although it seems unlikely for such a deeply religious woman, Ælfthryth was credited with masterminding the regicide so that her son could become king and she his regent – which is exactly what transpired. So terribly wicked was Ælfthryth that apparently when Æthelred expressed consternation at the cold-hearted assassination of his brother and king, she beat him black and blue with a candlestick.

Ælfthryth ruled on behalf of her young son until about 985, by all accounts with an iron fist. There was a deep-seated resentment towards both her and Æthelred however, that would swell up after her death. She was charged with the raising and education of Æthelred's sons by his first wife; the eldest – Æthelstan – was to remember her fondly in his will. She retired to a nunnery in Hampshire that she had founded and died sometime between 999 and 1001.

It's no exaggeration that – if Ælfthryth was instrumental in the death of Edward the Martyr – she changed the course of the English monarchy. It could be argued that without the tensions that derived from this action – and subsequent heightened unpopularity of Æthelred – there might never have been a Danish, followed by a Norman, invasion. Regardless of her personal unpopularity and the scandals and sins she may or may not have been guilty of, she was a technically admirable ruler as regent for her son and without a doubt surpassed the limitations of her sex and time. More people should know her name – which was probably pronounced something like 'Alf-frith', by the way..!

Emma of Normandy

Emma of Normandy (c.985–6 March 1052) was a princess of Viking blood, and queen consort of England twice over, as well as Denmark and Norway.

As the daughter of the Duke of Normandy, Emma was always going to show her worth in the marriage market. At the age of eleven or twelve she was shipped off to England to marry its king, Æthelred Unraed, the poorly counselled, the symbol of a new partnership of kingdoms united against Viking threat. The Vikings were kin to the Normans – Emma's own great-grandfather, Rollo, had been the Viking who originally founded Normandy (named after the 'North Man') – and the Normans had historically offered trade, safe harbour, and a launching off point for the Danes to raid the British coasts.

Although often pictured as a tremulous greybeard, Æthelred was only in his mid-thirties, but he already had a wife and ten children to his name by the time his child-bride arrived. The pair were married in a Christian ceremony in Canterbury, but his sons by his handfast wife Ælfgifu of York (who had possibly only recently died) were to retain their places in the line of succession. To add insult to injury, Emma was made to adopt the good Saxon name Ælfgifu as her regnal name.

But at least she *had* a regnal name; unlike her predecessor, Emma was consecrated as Queen of England and given tracts of land, income and a certain degree of power and authority. Her name appears as a witness to numerous documents, although it was likely many years before she would have been able to follow the language – or the politics – of her realm. She did her duty as queen, providing Æthelred with two new sons, Edward (aka the Confessor) and Alfred, as well as a daughter, Godgifu.

However content Æthelred was with his second wife, it transpired that the match would do little to nothing to stem the flow of Viking raids. An uneasy status quo had been maintained by Æthelred paying off Sweyn Forkbeard, the King of the Danes, but, in 1002, perhaps mistakenly buoyed in confidence following his recent marriage to Emma, Æthelred ordered the wholesale massacre of all Danes who had settled peacefully in England. Legend holds that one such unfortunate Viking noblewoman was the sister of Forkbeard, and the Danish king, understandably, swore a swift and terrible revenge. The Viking raids of recent years paled into absolute insignificance against the massive and concerted invasion they now launched, overrunning most of the country before 1011 was out.

Æthelred sent Emma and their children to her kin in Normandy before following himself in 1013 – it was over, and Sweyn and his son Cnut had full control of England. But, after all that, Sweyn died five or so weeks into his term as English king, and his body was returned to Denmark. The Danes and Cnut tried for a seamless succession, but the Witenagemot council (a sort of Anglo-Saxon parliament) disagreed. They sent word to Normandy that Æthelred was welcome back, as long as he had learned his lesson and would try not to be so *unraed* this time around. A peeved Cnut wasn't having any of it, and attempted to restart his father's assault. This time however, Æthelred and the English saw them off, and Cnut slunk back to Denmark to lick his wounds and regroup.

And so Emma returned to take her place as Queen of England, leaving her three young children in Normandy with her brother. Æthelred's success was tinged with sadness; his eldest son and heir, Æthelstan, had just died. Emma, however, saw an opportunity here, and pressed her husband to name her eldest son, Edward (then a boy of around ten) as his new heir – after all, she was a Viking princess who had been joined to him in Christian marriage – his children from his first marriage were more or less illegitimate in the eyes of the Church. Æthelred must have been considering it, because his adult son, Edmund Ironside, kicked off, eventually rising up in rebellion against his father. To make matters worse, Cnut made a reappearance, but this did at least prompt Edmund to return to the family fold, eager to assist in the defence of London against the marauding Dane.

Æthelred died on 23 April 1016; he was buried at the original St Paul's Cathedral, but his grave monument and, indeed, location, was lost after the Great Fire of London. And so Edmund Ironside acceded to the throne at this pivotal moment in history – except, although the Londoners called for him, the Witenagemot declared for Cnut. The two kings were at an impasse, forced to accept a partitioning of the country which would remain in force until the death of one of the participants to the treaty (at which the whole would go to the survivor). Following the fashion set by both Forkbeard and Æthelred for dying inopportunely early, Edmund died a mere month after the agreement was set, and thus Cnut became ruler of a unified England.

Cnut set about consolidating his position, exiling and murdering any unfortunate Anglo-Saxon heirs (as you would). Emma however was still as great a marriage prize as she ever was, and so Cnut promptly shafted his handfasted wife and married the old king's widow, a neat and tidy link between regimes. It is this hopping into bed with the Danes, quite literally, which shades Emma as a curious, heartless sort. That this resulted in the more-or-less abandonment of her children by Æthelred (still in Normandy) for a fair portion of their lives has been cited as evidence of Emma being an unfeeling mother. The fact remains, however, that Edward and Alfred, two undisputed heirs of the dead Anglo-Saxon king, were allowed to live, where lesser heirs were executed without pause; Emma's second marriage seems to have saved her children's' lives. Through it, she would also become Queen of Denmark, and of Norway.

Whether or not it was a love match and elopement, or Emma was forced into the marriage against her will, as it transpired Emma and Cnut ended up rubbing along reasonably happily together. Savvy Emma had learned from her experience with Æthelred and negotiated that any children she had with Cnut would take precedence over the children had had already had with his handfasted wife. And so, when Cnut died in 1035 Emma immediately moved to secure the treasury for her son, Harthacnut. Unfortunately, Harthacnut was in Denmark, but Cnut's elder son Harold Harefoot was there on the ground and it wasn't long before he was declared king by the Witenagemot. Emma fled to Flanders.

There then appeared on the scene some familiar faces. Edward and Alfred, Emma's sons with Æthelred arrived from Normandy to challenge Harold Harefoot, although whether it was on their own behalf of on behalf of their half-brother Harthacnut isn't really clear. Either way, they were unsuccessful. Harefoot's supporters captured and blinded Alfred, causing him to die of his wounds.

Incensed by the murder of his half-brother, probably goaded by his furious mother, Harthacnut consolidated his forces for an invasion. As it transpired, it wasn't necessary. Harefoot fell ill, and the Witenagemot approached Harthacnut and offered up the throne. Emma returned to England, triumphant again. Her eldest son Edward was given the governance of Wessex. To help promote her half-Dane son's suitability for the English throne, Emma commissioned a biography of her life, the *Encomium Emmae Reginae*, a curious little book of half-truths and justifications, but nevertheless a critical source for the history of early eleventh-century English politics.

And one final time this story spins on the untimely death of a young king – after all that, Harthacnut only reigned for two years, and we end up back where we started, with an Anglo-Saxon son of Æthelred the Unready. Edward the Confessor ruled for almost twenty-five years. He never did really warm to the mother who had abandoned him as a child. Emma died ten years into her elder son's reign, and is buried in Winchester alongside Cnut and Harthacnut. Fifteen years later, her Norman-blooded and Norman-raised son apparently decided to leave his throne to his cousin, William, the Bastard of Normandy, thus ending the Anglo-Saxon-Danish tangle of pre-conquest English royalty.

Edith Swannesha

Edith Swannesha aka Ealdgȳð Swann hnesce – 'Edith [the] Gentle Swan' (c.1025–c.1086) – also known as 'Edith Swanneck' or 'Edith the Fair' – was the first wife and consort of Harold Godwinson, a famous beauty known for her gentleness and the pleasing paleness of her skin.

Edith had been Harold's common-law wife since they were both very young, married by the old Danish custom of a 'handfast'. This meant that the Catholic Church – its influence on the rise in the British Isles – did not recognise the union as legal and saw Edith as more of a concubine than anything approaching a queen. Their many children however weren't considered illegitimate; one daughter in particular, Gytha, was known and addressed as 'princess' and married off to a Slavic Grand Duke.

Nevertheless, after Harold became king in 1066, he was prevailed upon to make a legitimate and Christian marriage and he did so with Edith of Mercia, the widow of the Welsh King Gruffydd ap Llywelyn, whom he had defeated in battle. This marriage seems to have been one of political convenience, and there was apparently no issue from it and after Harold's defeat at the Battle of Hastings, Edith of Mercia's brothers came and whisked her away and into the mists of history.

Edith the Fair, meanwhile, travelled to the bloody battlefield in Hastings. Harold's corpse had been brutalised and mutilated, and lay in the mud amongst countless others. The estimates are that 4,000 Saxons, 2,000 Normans and some 750 horses lay slain in that field in Senlac. The Normans refused – despite the pleadings of Harold's mother and his family – to surrender the body for burial, even after being offered the customary 'weight in gold'. Although she was assured that the body of her husband was disfigured beyond even her recognition, Edith walked through the carnage of the battlefield for hours until she recognised the torso of her lover by marks on his chest 'known only to her'; these are sometimes considered birthmarks, and sometimes love bites remaining from the couple's last passions the night before the battle. Some who are perhaps more patriotic than romantic claim it was a tattoo that said 'ENGLAND' across his heart.

Nobody knows what happened to Edith after the Normans took full control of England. It is likely she went into exile with her mother-in-law and children – maybe even to Kiev with her daughter Gytha – or perhaps she remained in England and entered the safety of a nunnery. The rich lands that records like the Domesday Book showed she had held in her own name were passed to prominent Normans. However, rather wonderfully, the descendants of Edith's daughter, Gytha, eventually ended up marrying into most of the Royal Houses of Europe – including back into England's; in fact, our current Queen Elizabeth is the 29th great-granddaughter of this famous Anglo-Danish beauty.

St Margaret of Wessex

Margaret of Wessex (c.1045–16 November 1093) – known posthumously as Saint Margaret of Scotland – was an English princess who was born in exile and became queen-consort of Scotland. Known for her piety and praised for her charitable works in life, she was canonised as a saint of the Roman Catholic Church in 1250.

Margaret was the grand-daughter of Edmund Ironside, the Anglo-Saxon King of England. When the Danish Cnut conquered England and took the throne in 1016, Ironside's toddler son – the Ætheling (or 'prince') Edward – was exiled. Edward grew up sheltered in the courts of Eastern European monarchs, and when he came to adulthood he travelled to Hungary, where he became a staunch and effective supporter of its king, Andrew I. Edward and his wife had two daughters and a son, who became the new Ætheling – Edgar – the last born male to the Royal House of Wessex.

Margaret's early childhood in Hungary was a simple and religious one. Their family's patron, Andrew I, was known as 'Andrew the Catholic' – famed for his extreme piety and loyalty to the Roman church – and it seems that this made a large impression on the young Margaret. When she was still just a child, her father Edward was recalled to England as a possible successor to his uncle, the heirless Edward the Confessor. Rather unfortunately, he died pretty much immediately after his arrival. No evidence survives that this was foul play, but it does feel rather convenient for all the rival heirs…

Still, Edward the Ætheling had come with a spare in the form of his son Edgar, so Margaret and her family were invited to reside at the English court. When Edward the Confessor died in 1066, Edgar was still way too young to be a viable option for king, resulting in the selection of Harold Godwinson. Hope still wasn't fully extinguished for the little prince – when Harold was defeated and killed by Norman invaders a couple of months later, Edgar was declared King of England. Of course, when the triumphant Normans marched on London, little 'King' Edgar was offered up like a sacrifice, and

William the Conqueror promptly prince-napped him and took him back to Normandy. Margaret's mother gathered up her two little daughters and fled.

Margaret's mother succeeded in getting passage on a ship back to the continent, but a storm drove them north where they were forced to disembark in Scotland and seek the protection of the King of Scots, Malcolm III (the son of murdered Duncan, of Shakespeare's *Macbeth* fame). The spot where the royal ladies are said to have blown ashore is still known today as Saint Margaret's Hope.

For King Malcolm, this was a windfall indeed. A widower, he was eager to marry one of the few remaining members of the illustrious Anglo-Saxon royal family and so took young Margaret as his wife. He had spent some time in the English court after the murder of his father, and so may have had a pre-existing acquaintance with Margaret and her family. The marriage was a successful one, resulting in six sons and two daughters. Margaret seems to have been indulged by her much-older husband, whose pagan temperaments she calmed by introducing him to religion and offering composed and enlightened advice. She worked tirelessly to bring the Scottish Church in line with those on the continent she had known in her childhood, which benefited the common people greatly.

Even in her private life, she remained extremely devout. She served food to orphans and washed the feet of the poor every day. A cave on the banks of the Tower Burn in Dunfermline was used by her as a place of devotion and prayer. She influenced her husband to support the cause of her brother, Edgar the Ætheling although his support was ineffectual and ultimately ended in tragedy; both Malcolm and their eldest son were killed in the Battle of Alnwick, against the English, in 1093. Margaret – not yet fifty years old – was stricken to the core with grief and died just three days later. With respect to her great personal devotion and what she and this had meant to Scotland, she was canonised as a saint some century and a half later.

Putting aside Margaret's undoubtedly selfless and virtuous personality, she was simply a great agent for social change in eleventh century Scotland. For generations she was held up as the very pinnacle of queenship. Even after her death, her achievements were compounded and her approach continued on through her three sons who each reigned as King of Scotland. Margaret really was a bit of a melting pot for the British Isles – a Saxon Princess with a continental up-bringing, mixing blood and ideology with that of the Celtic royals and, through her daughter Matilda, who married Henry I of England, on into the Norman line too.

Matilda of Scotland

Matilda of Scotland (c.1080–1 May 1118), born Edith of Dunfermline, was queen consort of Henry I of England.

Daughter of the King of Scots, Malcom III (he whose victory signals the end of Shakespeare's *Macbeth*) and his wife, the Anglo-Saxon princess now known as Saint Margaret, it seems the young Edith was always destined for a lofty position. The story goes that, during her baptism service, the royal baby pulled off the headdress of her godmother, Matilda of Flanders, then Queen of England, and it was seen as an omen that that position would be hers, one day.

The little princess's fortunes peaked and troughed – her father, brother and mother all died within in the space of three days and as a result the young girl was rather lost in the succession squabble that followed. She had once had noblemen lining up for her hand in marriage, but, following her parents' deaths, the teenaged Edith simply walked out of the abbey where she was being raised one day and did not return. For seven years she is simply absent from the records. But, in 1100, she reappeared in great style.

Henry I had found himself on the throne of England after the unexpected death of his brother, William II, and immediately proposed marriage to Edith. It was a no-brainer – Edith's brother Edgar was then the King of Scots, and Edith's Anglo-Saxon royal blood (she was descended from Alfred the Great) lent a touch of legitimacy to Henry – by now they were three kings in, but the Normans were still the johnny-come-latelies, after all. But legend likes to hold that it was the English royal family who had harboured the Princess Edith during her mysterious disappearance, and that she and Henry were well acquainted, even going so far as to claim that the marriage was a love-match. English Chroniclers of the time claimed that Henry had 'long been attached' to Edith, and even that he 'adored' her.

Edith and her younger sister had been educated in a series of English convents – she was famously pious (which one might expect from the daughter of a *literal* saint). In fact, most people believed that she had gone the whole hog and taken holy vows to become a nun – rather an obstacle to marriage. The argument was that when parents send their daughters to be raised in convents they usually expect them to become nuns, and, indeed, it seem that Edith had been sighted wearing a nun's black habit on occasion. Edith refuted the allegations. Her aunt had been the abbess of the convent in question and had apparently insisted upon her royal nieces wearing nun's veils so as to protect them from 'the lust of the Normans'. The council of bishops who had been called to decide the matter concluded in the lovers' favour, and Henry and Edith were married. Upon this marriage, Edith was rechristened Matilda, a much more suitable name for a Norman Queen. Edith – or, indeed, any other Anglo-Saxon name – was a bit too rustic for a Norman noble. In fact, the nobles gently mocked Henry and Matilda by referring to them as Godric and Godiva (typical 'English' names from before the Conquest) for their terribly un-Norman disinterest in fashion, partying or anything approaching style.

Needless to say, Matilda continued a pious lifestyle; she did all that was expected of a Christian queen, and more. She founded leper hospitals, wore hair shirts and attended church services barefoot. She kissed the sick and washed the feet of the poor. However, her top-notch education led her to becoming a great patron of the more modern arts and new sciences. She filled her household with musicians and poets and commissioned a biography of her revered mother. She had a keen interest in architecture and was involved with the building of numerous abbeys and bridges. Trusted implicitly by her husband, Matilda acted as Regent of England during Henry's periodic absences. In fact, after the first few years of their marriage, Matilda appears to have preferred staying behind at the Palace of Westminster and getting on with the business of governing rather than travelling with Henry, particularly after she had done her duty by him and provided him with a princely son, William (and a princessly daughter, another Matilda). The marriage seems to have become mostly a friendship rather than a romance by this time, but Henry didn't seem to mind, keeping very busy with his mistresses – he holds the record for the number of illegitimate children, with a number somewhere between 20–25 of them.

Matilda died in 1118, still only in her thirties. Despite his obvious penchant for the ladies, Henry genuinely mourned his queen, and seemed unwilling to remarry. All that changed when, eighteen months after her death, Matilda's son William drowned in the shipwreck of the *White Ship*. Suddenly heirless, Henry married again in a hurry, desperate to father another legitimate son. When his new queen failed to conceive, Henry decided he had to throw in his lot with his one remaining legitimate child, Matilda, who had been away in Germany and married to the Holy Roman Emperor since she was a small child. The Emperor had since died, leaving Matilda a 23-year-old widow, prime for remarrying, and, perhaps, more. Henry quickly wed her to the teenaged Duke of Anjou and gathered his household and council, making all swear a collective oath of allegiance to Matilda, and to recognise her as Henry's heir. Of course, this didn't exactly go to plan, leading England into a period known as the Anarchy where Matilda and her supporters quite literally battled with her cousin and rival claimant, Stephen of Blois. Still, examples of Matilda's skill in governance certainly harkens back to her extremely capable mother, a woman sadly rather overshadowed by a literally sainted mother before her, and a warlike daughter following after.

One place where Edith/Matilda is not forgotten however is in the words to the traditional nursery rhyme, *London Bridge is Falling* Down; legend has it that, due to her proclivity for building bridges over tributaries to the Thames, she is the 'fair lady' referred to at the end of every verse.

Nest ferch Rhys

Nest ferch Rhys (c.1085–c.1136) – or Agnes, daughter of Rhys – was a Welsh princess from the High Middle Ages.

She was the eldest legitimate child of Rhys ap Tewdwr, the last King of Deheubarth, by his wife, Gwladys ferch Rhiwallon ap Cynfyn, herself a princess of Powys. Both Deheubarth and Powys were minor kingdoms (or principalities) in Western Wales. Deheubarth was founded around 920 and flourished until Rhys ap Tewdwr's demise in 1093.

The Normans had arrived in Britain in 1066 and change was afoot; William II, Duke of Normandy was crowned William I of England on Christmas Day and proceeded to march west to conquer the British Isles. The inclement weather and tribal feuds of Dark Ages Wales proved too much of a hassle for William however, who only pushed as far as Offa's Dyke before deciding he didn't really fancy it, formally acknowledging the sovereignty of the Welsh princes, including Rhys ap Tewdwr.

When William died in 1087, his son, William Rufus ('the red') took the throne as William II. He was not content to have his kingdom end at Offa's Dyke as his father had been, and he had his barons invade Wales, leading to a decade of war. In 1093, Rhys ap Tewdwr was killed in battle and the young Nest and her mother were seized as hostages by the victorious Normans.

Although Nest would only have been around twelve or thirteen at this point, by all accounts she was already a beauty. A virgin Welsh princess of twice-royal parentage was a valuable pawn indeed, so it is not surprising that she was taken into William's court, where she immediately caught the eye of his famously lascivious brother, Henry.

The future Henry I – Henry 'Beauclerc' – is famous for his record twenty illegitimate children. Despite his obvious potency, somehow Henry ended up with no legitimate male heir when his son, William, was drowned in a shipwreck in 1120. He made his barons swear fealty to his only surviving legitimate child, a daughter, Matilda, although when he died they crowned her cousin, Stephen of Blois, instead. Matilda and Stephen engaged in civil war for almost twenty years, each controlling different parts of England at different times. This struggle, known as 'The Anarchy', only came to peace when Matilda's eldest son was named Stephen's heir after the death of his own; Matilda's son went on to become the famous Henry II (husband of the glorious historical-fiction favourite, Eleanor of Aquitaine).

Nest had a son with Henry, Henry FitzRoy (c.1103–58), one of Matilda's numerous half-brothers, at some point after which she was married off to William II's governor in the strategically crucial province of Pembroke, Gerald de Windsor, giving this Norman overseer legitimacy in the eyes of the fiercely patriotic Welsh. Gerald and Nest seemed to have a quietly contented marriage which resulted in four children; two of their children carried Norman names, William and Maurice, and two Welsh, David and Angharad.

In 1109, Cadwgan ap Bleddyn, Prince of Powys, gave a feast at his court in Ceredigion. At this feast, legend holds, Cadwgan's son Owain was told of the great beauty of Nest, who was staying in her husband's castle of Cenarth Bychan (possibly modern Cilgerran Castle), relatively nearby. One night during Christmas 1109, Owain and his companions and men-at-arms dug a tunnel underneath the gate of Cenarth Bychan in their fervour to get at Nest.

Fearful for her husband's life, Nest begged Gerald and his men to escape down one of the lavatory shafts cut in the walls of the castle from their bedroom's garderobe. Owain broke through to the bedroom only seconds later. He raped Nest in front of her children before setting fire to the castle and abducting them all.

This barbaric treatment of Nest invoked the rage of the Normans, especially that of Nest's old lover, now Henry I. He summoned Cadwgan's many rivals and offered them all of Powys if they could rescue Nest and avenge Gerald. With all this pressure on him, Owain first released Nest's children and then finally Nest herself, before fleeing to Ireland, with even his disgusted father denying him protection. Legend has Nest bearing two sons by her rapist during the time he held her captive, although these individuals do not appear in Welsh genealogies.

Nest's younger brothers – who had been spirited away for their protection after the death of their father – now returned from overseas, rising in rebellion against the Normans. It was a Welsh civil war as well as one between the Welsh and the Normans. Owain recklessly returned from Ireland to get involved, eventually earning Henry I's pardon for his crimes. Owain was ordered to rendezvous with the rest of the Norman force to proceed against one of the strongest Welsh rebel princes. En route, he and his force happened upon Gerald de Windsor and his men. Despite Owain being a royal ally, Gerald must have thought God was smiling upon him. He chose to avenge his wife's rape, and immediately turned his archers on Owain, killing him with a shower of arrows.

Gerald died in the 1120s, and the widowed Nest – apparently still not too old for childbearing – was married off by her sons to the Norman constable of Cardigan, with whom she had another two children whilst in her forties.

The story of Nest became quite popular in the nineteenth century, with her abduction and the civil war that followed earning her the appellation the 'Helen of Wales'. She was accused of having connived with Owain and gone with him willingly. Her pre-marital relationship with Henry Beauclerc was magnified into her having dallied with half of the Norman court. She's also credited with more illegitimate children than could be physically possible. With all her actual offspring, it's not hard to see how half of Wales can claim descendancy from Nest.

Gwellian ferch Gryffydd

Gwellian ferch Gryffydd (c.1100–36) was a beloved Princess of the Welsh, who fell leading her own army into battle against the Normans.

Gwenllian was the youngest daughter of the Prince of the Welsh kingdom of Gwynedd. A descendant of the High Kings of Ireland, Gwenllian was said to be bright and beautiful, a striking red-head. It's no wonder then that, in 1113, when Gruffydd ap Rhys, the Prince of Deheubarth visited Gweynedd he fell in love, and the pair eloped back to Deheubarth.

Early twelfth century Deheubarth was not an easy place to rule. The Normans were desperately trying to encroach further and further upon Welsh land, and already there were Norman castles being built on land that had once belonged to Deheubarth. In time honoured Robin Hood and Maid Marion fashion, the royal couple led raiding strikes against the Normans on the border, redistributing their wealth amongst the suffering locals. As a result, Gruffydd, Gwenllian and their four young children were often on the run or closed up in remote strongholds.

In 1136, Gruffydd was away, visiting Gwenllian's father in order to negotiate more support against the Normans. Said Normans seized their chance, leading violent raids against the local population of Deheubarth. Gwenllian had no choice, she had to raise and lead an army in their defence. The professional soldiers were elsewhere – Gwenllian had nobody but her two elder sons and two hundred or so local labourers. She tried to arrange one of the guerrilla-style raids she and her husband were known for, but was betrayed by one of her own chieftains, who gave her position away, and the Normans fell upon the Welsh without mercy. One of her sons was slaughtered trying to protect her, and the other was held back and made to watch as Gwenllian was felled, captured and beheaded right there in the middle of the field.

The furious Welsh raised up against the Normans in what became known as 'The Great Revolt'. Gwenllian's brothers themselves invaded and repossessed many tracts of previously Welsh, then Norman-held land, slaughtering the Normans they found there with all the mercy that had been shown their sister. For centuries after her death, Welshmen cried out 'Revenge for Gwenllian!' when engaging in battle. The field where she was killed is still known today as Gwenllian's Field (*Maes Gwenllian*) and it is said that a spring erupted from the spot on which her blood was spilled. For many generations, people claimed to see the headless ghost of the warrior princess walking in the field in which she died. Through her descendants, Gwenllian became ancestress to the House of Tudor.

Joanna Plantagenet

Joanna Plantagenet (October 1165–24 September 1199) was the seventh child of Henry II of England and his infamous queen consort, Eleanor of Aquitaine. During the course of her life she was a princess of England, the Queen of Sicily and the Countess of Toulouse.

Being the youngest of the royal couple's three daughters, Joanna spent her youth at her mother's courts at Winchester and Poitiers and didn't seem to have much to do with her father. She did however spend periods of time in the company of her various brothers, who are noted by contemporaries to have been fond of their little sister. In 1176, William II of Sicily sent ambassadors to the English court to ask for Joanna's hand in marriage. The ambassadors reported back that the young Plantagenet princess was a beauty, with strawberry blonde hair and fine features and was already well versed in languages, music and household management. The betrothal was confirmed and little Joanna set sail for Sicily.

After a hazardous voyage, Joanna arrived safely, and – on 13 February 1177 – she married King William and was duly crowned Queen of Sicily. She was just twelve, her husband twenty-three. The couple had one son, Bohemond, born in 1181; Bohemond disappears completely from the historical record so it's likely that he did not survive infancy. As a result, the direct line of Norman-Sicilian Kings through William II died out when William died suddenly in November 1189.

William's only potential heir was his aunt, youngest child of the late King Roger II. This aunt, Constance, was at this time married to the Emperor Henry VI of Germany. But before the Empress could muster herself to claim her hereditary rights, the Sicilian crown was claimed by one Tancred who was – like William II had been – a grandson of Roger II; however, he was from an illegitimate branch and had no legal right to the throne. Tancred was however a master politician and had managed to garner favour and support from the tempestuous Norman-Italian barons.

Joanna naturally supported the legitimate and lawful heir, the Empress Constance. Joanna had been a good queen and was well-loved by the Sicilian people, both the nobility and the lay-folk. Fearing her substantial influence, Tancred clamped down on Joanna's freedoms, taking away her right to travel around the kingdom, seizing both her pension due to her as Queen Dowager and also the land and revenue therefrom that she had brought into her marriage with William. Joanna was a virtual prisoner.

By this time, Joanna's closest brother – Richard I ('the Lionheart') had succeeded their father as king and was incensed by this treatment of his sister, a Norman Queen. He detoured to Italy on the way to crusading in the Holy Land in 1190 where he demanded the return of his sister to her family along with every penny of her dowry. Tancred refused, and so Richard decided he'd spend the winter in Italy, seizing monasteries, castles and the entire city of Messina to highlight his military might and his deadly seriousness when it came to his sister. Tancred had no option but to return Joanna and her lands.

Richard was in the process of taking a bride, Berengaria of Navarre, a match that was championed by his mother Eleanor, as Navarre bordered her land of Aquitaine. Eleanor arrived in Messina with Berengaria in March 1191, but as it was the Lenten season the wedding could not take place. Richard put his young bride into his sister's custody when his mother returned to her estates and the two young women became close friends. Richard, Joanna, Berengaria and the rest of Richard's retinue set sail for the Holy Land.

Two days out to sea, Richard's fleet was hit by a terrible storm which destroyed several vessels and forced the ship carrying Joanna and Berengaria miles and miles off course; they became stranded on the island of Cyprus. Sovereignty of Cyprus at this time had been seized by a tyrant, one Isaac Comnemus, who must have thought his luck had come in indeed when he realised the importance of two of the passengers now in his control.

Richard meanwhile had made it to Crete where he restocked before sailing out immediately in search of his sister and bride. He sped to Cyprus where he quickly liberated the women, however he lost his treasure in the process. The indomitable Richard of course simply chased the piratical Isaac down and captured him. According to Cypriot tradition, Isaac begged Richard that he not be put in irons, which Richard magnanimously agreed to, before shackling him in chains of silver instead. He then declared himself ruler of Cyprus for good measure. Richard also seized Isaac's only child, a daughter, who goes nameless in all historical records. This daughter joined Richard's court, attached to the household of Joanna and Berengaria. After a time, both Isaac and his daughter were ransomed into the care of the Duke of Austria, who was a distant relation of theirs.

Richard and his entourage once again started for the Holy Land. They arrived in Acre (now Northern Israel) in June 1191. Joanna and Berengaria (now formally married to Richard and recognised as his queen) lived quite comfortably whilst the various Christian kings of Europe kept themselves busy. It was the capture of Acre that gave rise to the famous image of Richard, suffering from scurvy, picking off Moslem guards on the walls with a crossbow whilst being carried about on a stretcher.

The protracted warfare soon took its toll on both Richard and Saladin (Sultan of an empire that included Egypt, Syria, Mesopotamia, Hejaz, Yemen, and parts of North Africa) and they sought peace. At this time, Richard offered Joanna in marriage to Saladin's brother Al-Adil, with a view to making the pair joint rulers of Jerusalem. It seems that Saladin wasn't totally against the idea, but both Joanna and Al-Adil put paid to the plan very quickly, both stating that they could never marry someone with whom they had such religious differences. Crusader history might look very different had this Plantagenet princess taken co-rule of Jerusalem in her own right in the early 1190s …

European royalty began to consider Joanna with renewed interest. Richard had no legitimate children, so those who wished to make marriage alliances with his dynasty could only do so with his cousins, or – if they were lucky – siblings. Phillip II of France put in a suit for Joanna's hand but the marriage was blocked on the grounds of consanguinity; Phillip's father – Louis VII – was the first husband of Joanna's mother, Eleanor of Aquitaine.

Eventually, Richard settled Joanna on Raymond VI, Count of Toulouse, giving her generous dower lands. The pair married in October 1196; their marriage would go on to produce three children, the heir, Raymond, a daughter Mary and a second son who died shortly after birth.

The marriage however was not a happy one. Raymond did not treat Joanna with respect, nor did he expect their household to. He took a mistress (some say entered into a bigamous marriage with) – that same

Cypriot maid, daughter of Isaac Comnemus, previously of Joanna's household. In 1199, pregnant with her third child, Joanna was left alone to face a rebellion in her husband's lands. Exercising her powers as regent, she arranged to lay siege to the castle of the leader of the rebellious lords, but was betrayed at the last minute. Heavily pregnant, her life threatened, Joanna escaped and headed northward to where her brother Richard was at war in Normandy. She arrived safely, only to discover that her brother had just recently died. Her mother Eleanor was present and whisked Joanna away to safety at her court at Rouen.

Joanna was world-weary. As the final months of her pregnancy approached she prevailed upon her mother to let her be admitted to Fontevraud Abbey. Eleanor used her considerable influence to have the nuns take her in; it would usually have been totally inconceivable for a still-married, pregnant woman to be permitted into the Abbey. Joanna went into labour on 23 September; the boy lived long enough to be baptised Richard. Joanna herself died soon afterwards and was veiled as a nun on her deathbed and buried in the Abbey. She was only 33 years old and was well-mourned across Europe. Her son, the future Raymond VII of Toulouse, was to name his daughter in her honour and when he died, nearly 50 years later, he instructed that he was to be buried at Fontevraud too. His effigy is depicted as kneeling beside his mother, facing her, both praying on their knees at the feet of Henry II. Eleanor and the Lionheart himself are also buried in the same vault.

Joan, Lady of Wales

Joan, Lady of Wales known to the Welsh by her Welsh name, *Siwan* (c.1191–2 February 1237) was the wife and consort of the Prince of Gwynedd, Llewelyn the Great, who became the effective ruler of most of Wales.

Joan was a favoured (albeit illegitimate) child of the then Prince John, brother of Richard the Lionheart. Her mother, identified only as 'Clemence', was probably a noblewoman of Normandy, and Joan spent her early childhood on the continent. Joan's father became king of England in 1199 and, six years later, Joan was summoned from Normandy to be married to Llewelyn ap Iorweth, the ruler of the principality of Gwynedd, in North Wales.

This marriage was a diplomatic masterstroke. Llewelyn, only in his early thirties, was rapidly becoming a legend in his own lifetime – and a thorn in the side of his liege lord, John. Barely out of childhood, a young Llewelyn had taken up arms against his uncles in order to reassert his claim to Gwynedd. Now grown, he was consolidating his rule, and chaffing at the incursions of Norman noblemen across the borders of Wales, and this rancour was spreading throughout the other Welsh kingdoms. In one move, John could tie this influential man to him in the most powerful way, through making him family. He also obtained a crown of sorts for his beloved, baseborn daughter.

For all that this was an incredibly practical marriage between two people of vastly different ages, nationality and loyalties, the marriage of Llewelyn and Joan seems to have been a happy one. Llewelyn was incredibly solicitous of his young wife. They sometimes resisted at Llewelyn's hunting lodge at Trefriw, where the nearest church was up a steep hill. Growing aware of Joan's fatigue, Llewelyn ordered a church built for her at the base of the hill. Although that church is long gone, one does still stand on the original site, and Joan and Llewelyn are the subjects of a set of stained glass windows there.

Joan proved invaluable to Llewelyn when, after a few years of partnership and allegiance, the prince spectacularly fell out with this father-in-law, resulting in John bringing together an alliance of all the other Welsh princes, as well as the Norman lords of the borderlands, and invading Gwynedd. Llewelyn's removal seemed certain, but as a last resort he sent Joan to negotiate with her father on his behalf. Whatever she said, it worked: Llewelyn did lose some land to the English throne, but he remained Prince of Gwynedd and to fight another day. And fight he did, regathering his power and his erstwhile allies amongst the Welsh kingdoms and striking back against John. In 1216, Llewelyn was affirmed as the leader of the Princes of Wales, with those men paying homage to him. He did not use the title 'Prince of Wales' (for all that was what he became), and so Joan was never the 'Princess of Wales', but rather became to be known as the 'Lady of Wales'.

History does not record how Joan felt with her husband and father entrenched against one another and near-constantly at war. Although you could forgive her some Norman loyalties, she had a vested interest in the future of Gwynedd and Llewelyn's position as de-facto Prince of Wales; her young son Dafydd, had been declared Llewelyn's heir, in precedent to his elder, illegitimate son, and Joan must have suffered from the conflict of interests between the will of her father and the interests of her husband and son.

King John died in 1216 and much of the political unrest in England died along with him. John had spent much of the end of his life in a civil war of sorts with his noblemen, who were so aggrieved with his governance that they even invited a French prince to come over to England and take the throne. The sins of the father however were not visited upon the son, the newly declared Richard II, a child of just nine, and tensions in England settled down, the majority of the rebels declaring allegiance to the boy-king.

Although she was much older than him, Joan seems to have enjoyed a good relationship with her half-brother. In the 1220s Richard, along with Llewelyn, petitioned the Pope in order to have Joan declared legitimate (on the technicality that neither of her parents had been married to other people at the time of her conception). Richard bestowed gifts of manors and lands on his half-sister and was (perhaps too) indulgent of Llewelyn when he quickly returned to old tricks and began harrying and invading along the Welsh/Norman borderlands.

It was during one such campaign that Llewelyn took as hostage a Norman noble, William de Braose. A member of a prominent border family, de Braose was utterly hated by the Welsh, who dubbed him *Gwilym Ddu*, or 'Black William'. While waiting for de Braose to be ransomed, it seems that the two men came to an accord, and Black William offered his daughter Isabella in marriage to Llewelyn's heir, Dafydd.

A year or so later, as the story goes, during the Easter festivities of 1230, Llewelyn returned from hunting to discover Black William in his bedchamber, and from the strength of his reaction it seems he was sure there could be no mistaking what was happening. He ordered that Black William be immediately hanged from the nearest tree, and the man was dragged to a field behind the castle and summarily strung up. Joan, his wife of some twenty-five years, was removed from court and put under house arrest, disgraced. But Llewelyn's ire, although it had flared swift and strong, burnt out surprisingly quickly. Within a year Joan was back in Llewelyn's good graces, and a few months after that, she was back by his side, returned to her position as Lady of Wales, the prince's apparent forgiveness of his consort's infidelity good proof that the pair enjoyed a strong and companionable marriage.

Joan died six years later, and Llewelyn was grief-stricken. He founded a religious house in her honour opposite what was said to have been Joan's favourite of their royal residences, Llanfaes. There Joan rested in her stone sarcophagus for the next three hundred years until another queen was accused for adultery, albeit this one paid the ultimate price. When Henry VIII began dissolving the Welsh monasteries he reached Llanfaes in 1537, and it was ransacked. Joan's bones were lost, the large sarcophagus used as a water trough for animals. It was almost another three hundred years before this rock effigy of the Lady of Wales was rescued, and established in a church in Beaumaris, Anglesey, where it sits today, the serene stone face of the woman Llewelyn the Great apparently could not live without.

Marguerite of France

Marguerite of France (c.1279–14 February 1318) was the first – but, of course, not the last! – French Queen of England, the second wife of Edward I.

Marguerite was the youngest daughter of King Philip III of France and his second wife, Marie, a daughter of the Duke of Brabant. Her royal father died when she was only three years old, and her half-brother duly took the French throne as Philip IV. We know little about the young princess's childhood, save that her upbringing was in the charge of both her devoted mother and her half-brother's queen, Joan (herself the queen regnant of Navarre).

Across the water in England, Marguerite's future husband was already over 40 by the time she was born, and had been the king, as Edward I, for almost a decade. The death of his beloved queen Eleanor in 1290 left him heart-sick and grief-stricken. Their marriage had been the stuff of romances and fairy tales; it was for her that the twelve 'Eleanor Crosses' were erected down the east of England, each cross marking a stopping point where the queen's body rested on its procession from Lincoln back to London. Unsurprisingly, the grieving king had no immediate stomach for a second marriage, but eventually it arrived on the metaphorical table.

With his finances and his army tied up with war with Scotland, Edward quite literally couldn't afford tensions to escalate with France. Seeking a diplomatic resolution, he suggested that his son marry a French princess. Philip IV proposed his half-sister Blanche, Marguerite's older sister. Blanche was apparently quite a catch – so much so that when he heard about her fabled beauty and charm, Edward decided he'd quite like to marry again after all. Philip agreed but it transpired that the lovely Blanche had been betrothed elsewhere all along. He then offered the younger sister Marguerite instead, but an incensed and humiliated Edward refused her for five years.

Eventually a double marriage was proposed – the king himself to marry the Princess Marguerite, and – in time – his son and heir would marry her niece, the three-year-old Princess Isabella. A handsome dowry was put forward for Marguerite, including the dower lands of the late Queen Eleanor. Edward's proxies, in France negotiating the terms of the unions, reported back that the now teenaged Marguerite was an ideal bride: beautiful, pious and virtuous although one can clearly see where Edward's focus lay, considering he asked his ambassadors for more nitty gritty details, such as the size of her feet and how thick her maidenly waist was.

Edward and Marguerite were married in Canterbury in September 1299 and – for all Edward was past sixty, and his new bride not quite eighteen – marital duties were duly fulfilled and Marguerite quickly fell pregnant (hardly surprising considering Edward's previous fecundity with his late wife Eleanor). Wife married and seeded, Edward hurried back to his Scottish campaign, in too much of a rush to even get a coronation organised for his new queen consort; in fact, nobody ever got around to crowning poor Marguerite, the first queen not to have been properly invested since the Norman Conquest. Despite this, she always styled herself with the full royal title in all her documents and correspondence, and certainly had two very fine crowns commissioned for her by Edward.

Marguerite was young, healthy and hearty. Despite an advanced pregnancy she chose to travel to be with Edward in the north, which delighted him – possibly it reminded him of his dear Eleanor, who had often accompanied him when he rode off to war. So energetic was this young queen that she was actually out hunting when she went into labour. A doting, delighted Edward flew 'like a falcon' to his wife's side and showered her and the new baby prince with gift after gift. The little prince was followed by another, and also a short-lived daughter.

Marguerite was still a very young woman, and could be seen as carefree and extravagant. She enjoyed music and comforts, as well as spending a literal fortune on fashion. Her husband indulged her and settled all her debts, the two seemingly getting on very well together. For all Marguerite clearly had a frivolous side to her nature, she took her roles of mother and queen very seriously. Her key role was in intercession; she once obtained a pardon for the entire city of Winchester when an important hostage managed to escape from there, calling down the king's wrath upon its citizens. She often interceded with the king on behalf of her stepson, Edward of Caernarfon (the future Edward II). Although she was only a handful of years older than the prince, she did appear to feel maternal towards him and he wrote to her often, sometimes requesting that she 'work' on his father to procure something for him.

The relationship between the heir and his father was a strained one. The king decried the influence of the prince's 'favourite' – Piers Gaveston – with whom the young Edward rode rampant across the kingdom. Prince Edward received a right royal grounding – his household was disbanded and he was sent away to Windsor Castle to think about what he'd done. While he was there, he petitioned Marguerite to get his father to calm down and restore his court to him. Marguerite duly obliged and Edward thanked her: 'We know well that this was done at your request, for which we are dearly grateful to you, as you know.'

Not long after this intercession, in 1307, Edward I died – with Marguerite by his side. The new widow, still only in her mid-twenties, could have had a whole second life but chose, for whatever reason, to remain unmarried and in England. Romantic legend has it that she declared that when Edward died, all men died for her. Now she could focus on protecting the interests of her young sons. Once Edward II ascended the throne he immediately revoked the exile of Gaveston and, before he'd even arrived back in the kingdom, had invested him with the title Duke of Cornwall. This was blindingly insensitive; Cornwall was a royal earldom and had been intended for one of his half-brothers, Marguerite's boys. Marguerite perhaps also stayed on in England to assist the new queen, Isabella, her little niece, now finally grown enough – at twelve – to fulfil the other half of the English/French marriage alliance that Edward I and Marguerite herself had begun years before. Marguerite was even present at the birth of the future Edward III.

Marguerite died on Valentine's Day 1318 at her castle in Marlborough, to which she had retired. She is overshadowed by both her predecessor Eleanor – who is remembered as the true love of Edward I's life – and her successor, her little niece, who would soon become the infamous She-Wolf of France and depose her unpopular husband, with both of Marguerite's sons allied at her side.

Isabella MacDuff

Isabella MacDuff (c.1285–c.1313) is a heroine of the Wars of Scottish Independence, a series of military campaigns between the English and the Scottish in the latter part of the thirteenth and early part of the fourteenth centuries. She was the daughter of the Earl of Fife and became the Countess of Buchan by marriage.

Only months after Isabella was probably born, the Scottish king Alexander III died, leaving as his heir his four-year-old granddaughter, Mairead/Margaret, the 'Maid of Norway'. Mairead was a Princess of Norway, the daughter of Eric II and Alexander III's daughter, Margaret.

Her panel of regents – the 'Guardians of Scotland' – agreed in 1290 that Mairead should marry Edward of Caernarvon, the son of England's Edward I. The Scots insisted, however, that this marriage did not create a union between the two hostile countries; Scotland was to continue to be considered wholly and legally separate from England.

Little Mairead set off to journey from Norway to her new kingdom; she landed on the Orkney Islands in September 1290 and promptly died, leaving thirteen rival heirs to the Scottish throne. The two major challengers were Robert Bruce, 5th Lord of Annandale (grandfather of the future Robert the Bruce) and John Balliol, Lord of Galloway. Fearing the civil war that was brewing between these two great Lords, the Guardians of Scotland wrote to Edward I, asking for him to mediate. Edward agreed, on the proviso that he be recognised as the 'Lord Paramount of Scotland'. With no leader, no army, and all of its nobility at one another's throats, Scotland had no choice but to agree to this unpalatable demand.

Edward moved swiftly, demanding homage and taking control of Scotland's royal castles and estates; he did, however, take the matter of arbitration between Balliol and Bruce seriously, and managed the debate well. John Balliol was eventually declared king in 1292, however it was clear that Edward I firmly considered Scotland a vassal state. Balliol was instructed to provide men and finance for England's war with France. However, he decided to throw in his lot with France (honouring the 'auld alliance' between the two countries) so Edward I duly declared war on Scotland. Thus began the Wars of Scottish Independence (of 'Braveheart' fame: 'FREEEEEEDOM!').

In 1296, John Balliol abdicated the throne after an embarrassing run of military defeats. Edward I had removed the 'Stone of Destiny' from Scone Abbey, the stone upon which the monarchs of Scotland had been crowned since time immemorial. Scotland finally seemed to have been conquered, and the war settled down to an uneasy simmer. The Stone of Destiny was kept in Westminster Abbey thereafter, and was incorporated into the coronations of the English – and then British – Kings and Queens. Since 1996, however, it has been returned to Scotland and is kept in Edinburgh Castle, with provision to transport it back to London when it is required for the next monarch's coronation ceremony…

Back to the marvellous Isabella. Although Isabella's natural father died when she was very young, her mother remarried a Scottish Lord who was allied to the Bruce family. This – coupled with the fact that the Bruces were cousins to Isabella – shows how she grew up with an intense patriotism to Scotland and its independence and an equally strong loyalty to the claim of the Bruces.

Unfortunately for Isabella, she was married off to John Comyn, the Earl of Buchan. Not only was Comyn about three times her age, but he was a supporter of the English *and* his family were cousins to Balliol and hereditary enemies to the Bruces. Hardly a match made in heaven. Myth holds that Isabella and the young Robert the Bruce were lovers, so to be shackled to someone who was pretty much the antithesis of him would have been rather torturous for Isabella.

Robert had not given up his hopes of the throne. In 1306, he met with his rival, John Comyn (a cousin of, not to be confused with, Isabella's husband). Their plan was to discuss who between them was best to lead Scotland, then the other would renounce their claims and offer their full support. It appeared, however, that Comyn had betrayed Bruce to the English, as a letter from him informing Edward I was intercepted. Robert slew the traitorous Comyn, uncaring in his rage that they were standing on the holy ground of the Kirk of Greyfriars Dumfries.

Knowing that he would become immediately excommunicated once the Pope heard of this murder, Robert had to act decisively. An excommunicated man can never be crowned king, so he had no choice but to try and outrun the news. He dashed for Scone Abbey, knowing that although the Stone of Destiny was gone, he still needed as much legitimacy of tradition as he could muster.

Cousin Isabella was in London when she heard the news. Another part of the Scottish coronation tradition was that the crown be placed on the monarch's head by the reigning Earl of Fife, the representative of Clan MacDuff, one of the oldest (and first to be legally recognised) clans of Scotland. The Earl of Fife was Isabella's younger brother Duncan, who had been a ward of the English court since their father's death. He grew up a contemporary of the prince (the future Edward II) and it is probably unsurprising that he may have held English sympathies. Either way, it was clear he could or would not travel to Scone to crown Robert the Bruce.

Legend has it that Isabella immediately made for Westminster Abbey, where she laid her hands on the pilfered Stone of Destiny where it lay installed underneath the throne. She then stole her husband's fastest horse and made for Scotland, the willing representative of Clan MacDuff.

Whether or not the poignant image of Isabella touching the Stone to imbue its power within her, and her headlong race on a stolen horse is true, we know for a fact that she arrived at Scone Abbey the day after Robert had been crowned Robert I. Robert was more than happy to go through the ceremony again and was duly crowned by a MacDuff.

Obviously, Isabella could not return to her home and husband after such an obvious and devastating act of defiance to England's cause. She was assimilated into Robert's household. Only months after the crowning at Scone, however, Robert was defeated at the Battle of Methven, so he made the decision to send Isabella and the rest of his female relatives north to safety. Isabella travelled with Robert's wife and queen, Elizabeth de Burgh, his young daughter Marjorie (from his first marriage) and his two sisters Christian and Mary. The royal women were betrayed by the Earl of Ross and given over to the clutches of Edward I.

The severity of Isabella's action in crowning and giving legitimacy to Robert the Bruce is illustrated in the harshness of her punishment. Edward ordered her to be sent to the castle at Berwick-upon-Tweed with these instructions: 'Let her be closely confined in an abode of stone and iron made in the shape of a cross, and let her be hung up out of doors in the open air at Berwick, that both in life and after her death, she may be a spectacle and eternal reproach to travellers.'

Isabella was imprisoned in this cage for at least four years. Although she had a privy and two maids to bring her food, she was exposed both to the elements and to the ridicule of the English. Perhaps most painfully of all – as Berwick was the most north-eastern town of England – she was left eternally looking out over her beloved Scotland where her cousin-king continued to fight against the yoke of the English, knowing that she may never be free to return to him.

After four years, Isabella was removed from the cage and given over to a friary. By this point, Robert the Bruce was at his height in terms of power and support, so keeping his female relatives alive and well was a tactical rather than a humanitarian move. However, when Robert's female relatives were returned to him in 1313 – during a hostage exchange for English nobleman taken after the Battle of Bannockburn – Isabella is not mentioned, suggesting that by this time she had died, perhaps – as she was still a relatively young woman – of the trials and stress her body had endured whilst hanging from the walls of Berwick Castle. Either way, she certainly deserves her accolades of Scottish martyr and heroine.

Robert the Bruce went on to force the English to sign a treaty recognising Scottish independence in 1328. His son and heir, David (II), married the sister of Edward III and there was peace between Scotland and England – for a time… However, whilst there were skirmishes and rebellions throughout the early reign of David II, Scotland remained an independent nation until the unification of Great Britain in 1707, and I'm sure Isabella would have been proud to know that her great act of defiance helped lead Scotland to freedom.

Marjorie Bruce

Marjorie Bruce or, if you prefer, de Brus, (probably 1296–1316) was the eldest daughter of Robert the Bruce, King of Scots.

Marjorie was named for her paternal grandmother, who had been Countess of Carrick, a figure who loomed large over the family. As the story goes, when a handsome young man arrived to inform the Countess that her husband had died on Crusade in the Holy Land, Marjorie was so enamoured with him that she held him captive until he agreed to marry her, which was certainly enterprising of her.

Marjorie Bruce's nineteen-year-old mother, the daughter of the Earl of Mar, died shortly after childbirth, leaving Marjorie motherless until her father married Elizabeth de Burgh when she was six. Two years later, Marjorie suddenly found herself a princess when her father declared himself King of Scotland on 27 March 1306. But there was no time to rest on newly-royal laurels. The crowning of the Bruce incensed the Scot's erstwhile overlord, the English King, Edward I, and he came down hard on his onetime vassals.

A beleaguered Bruce gathered up his family, sending them away for their safety. Marjorie travelled north along with her step-mother, aunts, and Isabella MacDuff (a Bruce loyalist who had fled her English husband to join his cause). The long-term plan was for the women to escape to Norway, where another of Marjorie's aunts was queen.

The English caught up with them at Kildrummy Castle and laid siege to it. The defenders were betrayed by someone in their own garrison, a blacksmith who set fire to the barns, making the castle undefendable. The ladies escaped, The Bruce's brother Neil remaining at the doomed castle, maintaining the defence for as long as he could to allow his kinswomen to get as far away as possible. Following their capitulation, the entire garrison was executed and Neil Bruce was given a full traitor's death – hanged, drawn and quartered.

Although they could have been forgiven for thinking they had got away, it wasn't long before Marjorie's party was captured by the Bruce-hating

Earl of Ross, who violated the laws of sanctuary by having the women arrested from the chapel in which they sheltered, immediately handing them over to the English.

For all his ire at the upstart Scots, Edward I balked at ordering the outright executions of the royal women, but he was firmly of the mind that they should be used to illustrate the price of rebellion against his crown. The women were separated. Marjorie's step-mother Elizabeth was a god-daughter of Edward I (indeed, he had arranged her marriage to the Bruce in an attempt to buy his good behaviour) and she was treated gently. In contrast, Isabella MacDuff and one of Marjorie's aunts, Mary, were imprisoned in cages. Edward had ordered the manufacture of an iron cage at the Tower of London for Marjorie, but – before she could be transferred to it – seemed to think again, perhaps advised against such treatment of a girl of nine. Instead, Marjorie was confined to the convent at Watton in Yorkshire, where she was kept in relative comfort, but solitary confinement, for the next eight years.

Meanwhile, the Bruce's star was rising and in 1314 he won a resounding victory at Bannockburn against Edward I's son and successor, by that time Edward II. The Bruce took a staggering number of English noblemen hostage, and – with these bargaining chips in hand – immediately demanded the return of his queen, daughter and sisters.

Eight years previously, the Bruce had sent his nine year old daughter north, and was now greeted with a seventeen year old returning from the south. A good portion of his wife Elizabeth's prime child-bearing years had passed while she was under house-arrest in England, and so Marjorie's importance as the Bruce's only child increased dramatically. Her uncle David had been and would remain the king's heir – Robert wasn't as forward thinking as all that to have his daughter succeed him on the throne – but Marjorie's task was now to produce a direct male heir for the Bruce dynasty.

With swiftness, the marriage was arranged, and Marjorie was wed to Walter, 6th High Steward of Scotland, who had been the proxy the Bruce had chosen to receive his family at the Anglo-Scottish border. Walter had distinguished himself at Bannockburn and it seems his reward was to include both large tracts of land and marriage into the royal family. It wasn't too long before Marjorie got on with her duty, falling pregnant after about a year of marriage, and this is where the sad, short life of Marjorie Bruce takes its final tragic turn.

As the story goes, a heavily pregnant Marjorie was out riding near Paisley Abbey on 2 March 1316 when her horse was suddenly startled, throwing her to the ground. The extent of her injuries was never documented, but what is known is that her child was born prematurely right there and then, and Marjorie died as a result, not yet twenty years old, a sad mirroring of her own mother's death in chidbirth at the same age. Legend holds that a primitive roadside caesarean was performed to save the life of the baby. Generations later, when Shakespeare's Macbeth hears the seemingly-impossible prophecy that 'none of woman born shall harm Macbeth' he later discovers that his adversary, Macduff, was 'from his mother's womb untimely ripp'd', an allusion – apparently – to the infamous way that Robert II entered the world.

Because Robert II he was. Marjorie's last words are reported to have been, 'He´s a laddie; I ken he´s a laddie; he will be king.' This improbable prophecy eventually came true, but not immediately; Robert was 55 when he succeeded his uncle David on the Scots throne (but he then ruled for a further twenty years!).

A cairn marks the spot called 'the Knock' near to where poor Marjorie Bruce reputedly fell from her horse, bringing to a close a short, sharp yet significant life. The descendants of Marjorie's son with Walter Steward became the House of Stewart, or Stuart.

Joan of Kent

Joan of Kent (1328–85) was a granddaughter of Edward I. She was lauded by her contemporaries as the most beautiful woman in all of England and is known to history as the 'Fair Maid of Kent'.

When she was just a babe in arms, her father – the Earl of Kent, the youngest son of Edward I – was executed for continuing to support Edward II against his marauding queen, Isabella – the She-Wolf of France – and her lover Roger Mortimer. She grew up a ward of William Montacute, one of Edward III's closest companions, with Queen Philippa also taking an interest in the girl's upbringing. Details of Joan's childhood are sketchy, but it seems to have been a happy one, despite the violence that had befallen her family when she was a baby. When Joan was 13, she was married off to Montacute's son and heir, another William, and took her place at court.

Joan is often credited with inspiring the foundation of the Order of the Garter. Legend has it that she was dancing at a court ball when her garter came loose and slipped down her leg onto the floor. Although nearby courtiers ridiculed and derided her, Edward III picked it up and returned it to her, proclaiming: '*honi soit qui mal y pense*' ('evil to them who evil thinks'), the phrase that is the motto of the Order to this day.

Several years after Joan's marriage however, a minor nobleman – Thomas Holland – returned from the Crusades and was made seneschal (or household steward) to the younger William Montacute. After a short while, Holland began petitioning the Pope, claiming that Joan had entered into a clandestine marriage with him the year before she had been given to Montacute, when she was but 12 years old. Joan was apparently in support of her return to Holland – legend has it that William Montacute locked poor Joan in a tower – and the Pope agreed, returning her to marriage with Holland. Poor Montacute, once bitten and twice shy, very circumspectly chose a six-year-old girl for his next bride, lowering the risk of previous, secret marriages!

Some historians suggest that the whole secret marriage was a lie concocted by Joan and Holland after he returned from the Crusades and took up his position as her seneschal; the two could have fallen in love and contrived the whole thing as an expedient way to free Joan from her ties with William Montacute. Either way, their marriage seemed to be a happy one. They had at least four children – whereas Joan and Montacute's marriage had been barren – with Joan being the only noblewoman of her generation to accompany her husband whilst he fulfilled his military duties. Holland, later created Earl of Kent, became one of Edward III's most trusted military commanders but in 1360, after eleven years of marriage, Joan found herself widowed.

Joan was in a difficult position. Although she had the respect and the finances inherited from her late father, the rumours and wrangling over her marital status had forever affected her reputation. Over a decade after her death, the chronicler Adam of Usk described Joan as 'given to many slippery ways'. Now in her thirties, Joan was still a remarked upon beauty; indeed, she was lauded as 'the most beautiful woman in all the realm of England' by the court historian Jean Froissart.

And waiting in the wings to snap up the beauteous Maid of Kent was Edward, the Black Prince, heir to the throne. The Prince, also in his thirties, had never been married before, despite being one of Europe's most eligible bachelors, which has given rise to the romantic tradition that he had loved Fair Joan since childhood and would not countenance marriage to any other. It certainly seems to have been a love match; the English-born twice-married mother of four was certainly no suitable match for the heir to the throne and the king, queen and even the Archbishop of Canterbury were against the pairing. Furthermore, the marriage was forbidden on the grounds of consanguinity – they were too closely related – and Edward had stood as godfather to Joan's sons with Holland.

Legend tells of a charming exchange between Prince Edward and the newly widowed Joan. Edward was discussing which, if any, of his friends and companions Joan would care to marry. Joan replied that had quite made up her mind to never marry again, as she was already in love with the most gallant man in the world, and to marry anyone else would be treason to her heart. Prince Edward pressed Joan into revealing the identity of her true love, which – of course – was he.

Probably figuring it had worked out okay for Joan the last time, it seems the couple entered into marriage regardless, forcing Edward III to resign himself to the situation and to petition the Pope for a papal dispensation to allow the couple to marry formally and legitimately, which was duly granted. Just to be one hundred per cent sure of the legitimacy of any heirs born, the royals sought a confirmatory dispensation from the Pope's successor too – and an elated Prince Edward donated a ridiculous sum of money to the Church in gratitude, which served to endow Canterbury Cathedral.

Their formal wedding took place in the chapel at Windsor in October 1361. The bride wore a red dress with cloth of gold, decorated all over with birds, and duly became the first member of the English royal family to bear the title of Princess of Wales. The marriage was a happy one. Edward, certainly, was besotted with Joan, spoiling her dreadfully and allowing her to spend lavish amounts of money. When he wrote to her, he addressed her with sweet phrases such as 'my dearest and truest sweetheart and beloved companion'. It is noted in contemporary records that they were very tactile and affectionate with one another, kissing and holding hands often. After their marriage, Prince Edward set up his own court in Aquitaine, and Joan bore him two sons in quick succession, Edward and Richard, the former dying young, the latter going on to become the much maligned Richard II, until his overthrow (and probable murder) by his cousin Bolingbroke (Henry IV), in the first 'act' of what would become known as the Wars of the Roses.

By 1370, the Black Prince's campaigning days were over. He had become affected by a mysterious and debilitating illness and this combined with the grief over his eldest son's tragic death led the royal couple to return to England. Such was Edward's infirmity that Joan was increasingly called upon to represent him publicly, and carried out this duty without reproach, maintaining excellent terms with everyone of importance at the royal court. This stood her in good stead when, in 1376, the Black Prince finally died, with the king dying the following year. Joan's and Edward's remaining son, Prince Richard, duly became King of England at the tender age of ten.

So the Fair Maid never became Queen of England, though evidence suggests she would have been an excellent one. She was adored by the English people; on her return from a pilgrimage to her late husband's tomb in Canterbury she was stopped by Wat Tyler, leader of the Peasants' Revolt movement. Not only was she allowed to pass unharmed but was saluted with accolades and kisses and provided with an escort for the rest of her journey home. Joan was heavily involved in her son Richard's upbringing, and had considerable influence while he was in his minority. While she showed interest in politics and issues of religion, she was careful not to tread on any toes, to be accused of inferring or nepotism, and the good relations that she had fostered with the rest of the royal family during her marriage to Edward kept the court on an even keel during the young king's minority. She often worked as a go-between and mediator for the king and his family – she was ever a natural peacekeeper and easy to love. Once she was satisfied that Richard had matured enough that he no longer needed her guidance and protection, Joan arranged his marriage before quietly retiring from court.

But the story of Princess Joan does not end happily. Her adult son from her first (second?) marriage, John Holland, was on campaign in Scotland when a brawl broke out, resulting in the death of the son of the Earl of Stafford, unfortunately a favourite of Richard's queen, Anne of Bohemia. As was the law, Richard sentenced his half-brother to death for the murder. Joan pleaded with her royal son tirelessly for four days. On the fifth day, she died suddenly, of unknown causes. A grieving Richard pardoned his half-brother as his mother would have wished, transmuting the sentence into a forced pilgrimage to the Holy Land. The chronicler Walsingham attributed her dramatic death to a broken heart at her failure to reconcile her two sons.

Even though the Black Prince had made space for Joan beside him in his crypt at Canterbury – even going so far as to commission carvings of his beloved wife's face to adorn the crypt's ceiling so he could stare up at her beauty for eternity – Joan specified in her will her desire to be laid to rest beside her first husband, Thomas Holland, in Lincolnshire. Where she might have been considered a touch scandalous at the point of her marriage into the royal family, some two and a half decades later she died widely loved and respected, a princess beyond reproach. Although her Plantagenet line of issue died out with the death of Richard II, through her children by Holland she is the ancestress of many English aristocratic families.

Margaret Drummond

Margaret Drummond (c.1340–c.1375) was the second wife and queen of David II of Scotland.

A member of the Scottish gentry, the young Margaret caught the eye of her king whilst he was married to Joan of the Tower, an English Princess – daughter of Edward II and Isabella of France. David and Joan's marriage was pretty loveless, even by contemporary standards. In 1357, when David was released after a spell imprisoned in the Tower of London by his brother-in-law, Edward III, Joan decided she was quite happy staying in London. She died in late 1362, leaving David a widower.

A few years later, on 20 February 1364, David took the Lady Margaret Drummond to be his new queen (her first husband having conveniently shuffled off this mortal coil by this point). By marrying his mistress, David raised the whole of Clan Drummond dangerously high, creating great resentment towards them. His 'love match' was unseemly, unprecedented; whilst Scotland was not the world power that say England or France could claim to be, David could still have picked his bride from a pool of European royal virgins.

However, it didn't turn out to be that much of a 'love match' after all. Barely five years after their formal marriage, David filed for divorce from Margaret, on the grounds of her infertility. This was rather rich coming from a man whose 37-year-long first marriage had also resulted in no children, whilst Margaret had had a son with her first husband – I think we're all in agreement that if there was any fertility issue at play here, it was more likely on David's side!

Margaret certainly seemed to think so and wasn't about to take the divorce lying down. She escaped the control of the king's men and travelled, incognito, to Avignon in Southern France, where the current Pope was residing. Said Pope agreed that there was no reason to consider she was infertile, and promptly reversed the divorce.

David was scuppered. He was stuck legally married to a queen who was now estranged from him and had no heir other than his sister's son. By 1369 he had picked up a new love of his life, Agnes Dunbar, but Margaret's appeal to the Pope left him unable to marry her. As it turns out, it was all moot, as David died unexpectedly in February 1371, long outlived by the queen he had embarrassed and scorned.

Eleanor Cobham

Eleanor Cobham, Duchess of Gloucester (c.1400–7 July 1452), was first the mistress and then the second wife of Humphrey, Duke of Gloucester, the youngest son of Henry IV. Eleanor was convicted and imprisoned for 'sorcery' and 'treasonable necromancy' in 1441 and forced to make a public penance in the streets of London – all this for a woman who came within a breath of being the Queen of England..!

The daughter of a minor noble, Eleanor was brought to court in 1422 to become a lady-in-waiting to the newly arrived Dutch noble Jacqueline, Countless of Hainaut – an illustrious woman whose impressive array of titles also included Duchess of Bavaria-Straubing, and Countess of Holland and Zeeland. Jacqueline was fleeing a disastrous marriage and was hoping that the English might help her wrest control of her territories back from her useless husband.

After the sudden death of Henry V and ascension of the infant Henry VI, Jacqueline fudged a divorce from her husband on the grounds of consanguinity and married the new king's uncle and Lord Protector, Humphrey – the Duke of Gloucester – and so it was that her lady-in-waiting, Eleanor Cobham, came into his sphere. A well-matched pair, the Duke and the lady became lovers around 1425.

Both attractive, pleasure-loving and ambitious people, they openly flaunted their relationship whilst poor abandoned Jacqueline languished on the continent. Humphrey was known to have had two illegitimate children – the wonderfully romantically named Arthur and Antigone Plantagenet – Eleanor could well have been their mother, but if she was, it is likely that Humphrey would have retrospectively legitimised them after their legal marriage took place.

In 1428 the Pope ruled that Jacqueline and Humphrey's marriage was invalid – she hadn't exactly dotted her i-s and crossed her t-s when it came to her 'annulment' from her first husband. Luckily for

Jacqueline, her ex was by then dead, and so there was absolutely nothing stopping Humphrey from marrying her again and making everything square and legit. Except that instead, Humphrey married Eleanor Cobham.

The new Duchess wasted absolutely no time making sure everybody understood her new status. She rode through the streets of London dressed up to the nines and accompanied by so many men at arms you would have been forgiven for assuming she was someone far more important than she actually was. Her contemporaries remembered her as proud and prickly – although the young Henry VI seems to have been fond of his aunt and gave her many presents.

In 1435, Humphrey's elder brother the Duke of Bedford died, which made Humphrey the heir presumptive to the still-young and childless Henry VI. Now this knight's daughter made good was heir to the Queenship of England! But the house of cards came tumbling down in 1441. A group of men were arrested for using 'astrological predictions' to forecast that Henry VI was soon to suffer a life-threatening illness. The men admitted their treason, but swore they had only done what they did on the instigation of the Duchess of Gloucester, who had hankered to know if it was likely her husband would ever sit on the throne.

A panicked Eleanor fled to Westminster, claiming the right of sanctuary. She might have hoped that her high status would save her from trial for treason; she was right, but nothing could stop the ecclesiastical courts trying her for witchcraft and heresy. A thorough investigation into Eleanor's life and movements threw up more and more damning evidence. A known 'witch' – Marjorie Jourdemayne – said that in the 1420s Eleanor had contracted her to produce love potions that would make the Duke of Gloucester marry her. Eleanor denied this, claiming that the potions had been to help her conceive. Nevertheless, she was found guilty, as were her co-conspirators, who were hanged, drawn and quartered or burned.

The Duchess' sentence was a forcible divorce from her husband, and a public penance through the streets of London before going on to life imprisonment. On a cold November day, shamefully bareheaded and dressed simply in black, Eleanor walked from Temple Bar to St Paul's Cathedral, where she offered up the wax taper she had carried to the altar. Two days later she did the same from Swan Pier to Christ Church, and then for a third time from Queenhithe to St Michael's. Each time

A 19th century depiction of a war-like Scota in a book of Irish history. (*Public domain*)

Above: Caractacus being delivered up to the Romans by Cartimandua, in an 18th century painting by Francesco Bartolozzi. (*Public domain*)

Left: Judith of Flanders with her third husband Baldwin, in this 19th century painting by Félix de Vigne. (*Public domain*)

The monument erected in 1913 to commemorate 1,000 years since the fortification of Tamworth by Ætehlflæd. (*Photographer Humphrey Bolton, Creative Commons*)

An unsuspecting Edward the Martyr about to be martyred, accepting a cup of mead from his stepmother Ælfthryth in this 19th century depiction from a a chronicle of early English history. (*Public domain*)

Right: Emma of Normandy Emma of Normandy and her two young sons; the Latin in the background details how she fled into Normandy with them. (*Public domain*)

Below: Edith discovers her lover's corpse on the battle field of Hastings in this 19th century painting by Horace Vernet. (*Public domain*)

A detail from this mural by William Hole in the Scottish National Portrait Gallery shows Malcolm greeting Margaret as she makes land at Saint Margaret's Hope. (*Public domain*)

Above: An intimate little detail from a medieval manuscript currently held in the British Library here shows Nest and Henry I in bed together, naked except for their crowns. (*Public domain*)

Right: Close up of the face of the sarcophagus effigy of 'Siwan', the Lady of Wales, which was ignominiously used as an animal water trough following the Dissolution of the Monasteries 300 years after her death. (*Author's own*)

This modern tableau at Edinburgh Castle shows the rebellious Isabella MacDuff crowning her cousin Robert the Bruce King of Scots at Scone in 1306. (*Public domain*)

A 19th century reimagining of the concept of the Ceremony of the Garter by Albert Chevallier Tayler, with Edward III picking up Joan of Kent's slipped garter. (*Public domain*)

Above: This 19th century engraving for a historical chronicle shows a penitent Eleanor Cobham after admitting she had requested the king's horoscope cast. (*Public domain*)

Right: Portrait of an unknown woman from the National Portrait Gallery, by an unknown artist, but traditionally known as Margaret Pole. (*Public domain*)

Detail from a larger oil painting from the Palace of Westminster by Frank Cadogan Cowper, showing a young Margaret Tudor with her younger brother, the future Henry VIII, at Eltham Palace in 1499. (*Public domain*)

A contemporary portrait of Mary Grey currently held in the Chequers collection, usually attributed to Hans Eworth. (*Public domain*)

Portrait by an unknown artist traditionally believed to be Mary Boleyn, sister of Anne and grandmother of Penelope Rich. (*Public domain*)

A contemporary portrait of Arbella Stuart as she looked in her later years, currently held by the National Gallery of Scotland and attributed to Robert Peake. (*Public domain*)

The unfortunate Sophia Dorothea of Brunswick with her children, painted around 1690 by Jacques Vaillant, before her fall from grace. (*Public domain*)

A stately portrait of the indomitable Queen Caroline, either very flattering or before she got so obese that she needed to be wheeled around the place. (*Public domain*)

A whimsical portrait of Maria Fitzherbert in around 1788, painted by Joshua Reynolds, currently held by the National Portrait Gallery. (*Public domain*)

The newlyweds Charlotte and Leopold at the opera before tragedy struck in this 1817 work by William Thomas Fry, currently held by the National Portrait Gallery. (*Public domain*)

there was a large crowd on hand to witness her disgrace and humiliation, eerily silent – they had been ordered not to molest the former Duchess, but neither were they to show her any respect. After this, Eleanor spent the last decade of her life imprisoned in various castles. It wasn't all bad – the soft-hearted Henry VI still sent her presents and allowed her 100 marks a year and a household of twelve people!

Although he must have once loved Eleanor fiercely, Humphrey never attempted to come to her rescue. Perhaps frightened of implicating himself, and all too aware of the great tensions around the Lancastrian court, Humphrey said nothing. He died in 1447 – apparently due to a stroke, although murder was rumoured at the time. Posthumously – and probably more in relation to the growing hard-feelings against Henry VI and his ministers than anything else – he became known as 'Good Duke Humphrey'. Eleanor was neatly forgotten about – we didn't know her date or even place of death until the 1970s.

In the end, Eleanor's legacy would be the catalyst for a change in the law. A year after her trial, Parliament declared that peeresses charged with treason were to be judged and executed the same way as everyone else – unfortunately for queens such as Anne Boleyn and Catherine Howard, a hundred years or so later.

So, was Eleanor Cobham a witch? Of course not. It was a fashionable court pastime to dabble in potions and predictions – not exactly accepted, but pretty normal. Eleanor was unfortunate in that she lived in a treacherous political climate that was soon to result in the War of the Roses, she was an over-reacher who wasn't well liked, and her husband was – to some – considered a political liability. It wasn't quite a stitch-up as she was technically guilty of everything she was accused of – but she was certainly the victim of political intrigue.

Margaret Pole

Margaret Pole, Countess of Salisbury (14 August 1473–27 May 1541), a 'Plantagenet Princess' who was executed by her cousin, Henry VIII.

A 'Wars of the Roses baby', Margaret was the only daughter of George, Duke of Clarence, the brother of Edward IV and Richard III. For all Margaret was born into the utmost privilege, her childhood was tumultuous to say the least. When she was three, Margaret's mother and newborn brother died, presumably from childbirth complications. Her father, who had never been of a particularly stable disposition, was convinced that one of her ladies-in-waiting had poisoned them, going so far as to execute the lady without due process. Clarence's volatility finally proved to be too much, slandering and scheming as he was against his previously tolerant elder brother, and he was executed for his treason in 1478 (rumour had it by being drowned in a barrel of wine, which has to be high up there on the list of exceedingly upper-class deaths). Forever stained by their father's attainder, Margaret and her brother Edward were denied their places in line for the throne but were kept within the care of the wider royal York family.

At the Battle of Bosworth, Margaret – by then in her early teens – lost her last remaining uncle in Richard III and she and her brother Edward were taken into the care of the new king, Henry Tudor, who was married to Margaret's first cousin, Elizabeth of York. Edward was kept closely confined to the Tower of London – as a York Prince, he was an obvious threat to this fledging Tudor dynasty – but Margaret was kept at court and treated gently. Eventually, the Plantagenet princess was Tudorised when Henry VII married her off to Richard Pole, whose mother was a half-sister to his own. In 1499, her brother Edward, who had been held in the Tower 'out of all company of men, and sight of beasts' (chronicler Edward Hall) since 1485, was finally executed. It's unclear why Henry VII finally decided to act in this way. Perkin Warbeck, who had claimed to be the younger 'Prince in the Tower', had been defeated and imprisoned (fittingly) in the Tower some eighteen months before, and it seems Edward may have – willingly or unwillingly – become embroiled in his escape plans. Rumour also has it that no European monarchs would consider marrying their precious princesses into the upstart Tudor family whilst the York heir lived. Certainly, after Edward's execution, Ferdinand of Spain sent his daughter Katherine to marry Henry's heir, Arthur, and Margaret became one of her ladies-in-waiting. Legend holds that the pious Katherine was haunted by this 'murder' she had caused for the rest of her life.

Prince Arthur died in 1502, as did Richard Pole two years later. With Katherine of Aragon's household dissolved after Arthur's death, Margaret found herself with no husband and no salary, with five young children. So dire were Margaret's finances that Henry VII had to pay for her husband's funeral costs. Margaret had no choice – she dedicated her middle son, Reginald, to the church and took herself off to live in Syon Abbey with the nuns. And there Margaret remained until Henry VII's death in 1509 and the ascension of Henry VIII. Henry had married his elder brother's widow, and Katherine immediately restored Margaret to her household. Margaret was on the up-and-up; Parliament voted to restore some of her family's lands and titles and Margaret became the Countess of Salisbury, one of only two women in sixteenth century England to be a peeress in her own right, the other being Anne Boleyn, as Henry VIII created her Marquess of Pembroke in preparation for their marriage. She proved herself an astute landowner, and by 1538 she was the fifth richest peer in England, marrying her children well and enjoying being a patron of new learning.

Once again Margaret's good fortune would be transitory. Like so many, she was swept up in the turmoil surrounding the king's Great Matter, namely his divorce from Katherine of Aragon and, by association, the Catholic Church. When Henry and Katherine's daughter Mary was declared a bastard in 1533, Margaret – who had been the princess's governess for almost ten years – would not accept it, stubbornly refusing to hand over Mary's plate and jewels when asked and begging the king that she be allowed to continue to serve Mary at her own cost (which was rejected). The son that Margaret had devoted to the church all those years ago, Reginald, by now the Dean of Exeter, had also refused to support the king's divorce, exiling himself to Europe and publicly speaking out against the proposed Boleyn marriage. Henry had hoped that his cousin would have been of use persuading the ecclesiastics of Europe that Henry and Katherine's marriage had been invalid only to find the opposite, and he was enraged. To make matters worse, support began to grow for a marriage between Reginald and Princess Mary, a couple with inarguably strong dynastic claims, mirroring what Henry VII had once done when he married Elizabeth of York, drawing both sides of the family together once more; although Reginald held many priestly positions, he was never formally ordained and thus could have married.

With Reginald out of his reach in Europe, an incensed Henry struck out at his family in England, arresting Margaret and two of her sons in November 1538. While Margaret had been stubborn when it came to Princess Mary and remained staunchly Catholic (refusing to let her household hear the mass in English), there is no evidence that she had actively supported action against Henry; indeed, she had written to Reginald scolding him for his 'folly'. Her interrogators fed back to Thomas Cromwell that although they had 'travailed with her' for many hours she would 'nothing utter,' and they were forced to conclude that either her sons had not included her in their plans for 'treason' or she was 'the most arrant traitress that ever lived'. They also admiringly told Cromwell that they felt her 'rather a strong and constant man, than a woman.'

A lack of evidence did not usually stop Henry (or Cromwell) from 'getting his man', and duly – six months after her arrest – Cromwell arranged for the 'discovering' of a banner portraying the five wounds of Christ in Margaret's belongings, allegedly proving her support for the Catholic Church and thus her son Reginald's ambitions on the English throne (it is the same emblem under which the Pilgrimage of Grace had marched against Henry). This was enough to get an attainder for Margaret's treason; she was stripped of her lands and titles and sentenced to execution at the king's pleasure.

Margaret resided at the Tower for two and a half years in relative comfort. Henry paid for her servants and afforded her a generous living allowance and his fifth wife Katheryn Howard, even sent Margaret some warm clothing when she complained of the cold – nobody, least of all Henry was keen to put an axe to the neck of this elderly princess. That changed with devastating swiftness. On the morning of 27 May 1541, a shocked Margaret was informed she was shortly to die. It was as much of a rush as it sounds; there was no scaffold ready, only a small ad hoc block had been improvised for her head. There had been more Catholic uprisings in the north; maybe Henry was finally incensed enough to remove this last big York thorn from his side.

Margaret was floored. She immediately argued that she hadn't been charged with any crime, so for what reason was she to die? She scratched words into the walls of her room, committing her protestations of innocence to the stone:

> For traitors on the block should die;
> I am no traitor, no, not I!
> My faithfulness stands fast and so,
> Towards the block I shall not go!
> Nor make one step, as you shall see;
> Christ in Thy Mercy, save Thou me!

Margaret was led out to the execution green at around 7am; as she was a peer, she was not executed before a crowd. There was certainly an audience though – both the ambassadors to the French and the Holy Roman Empire passed down written reports of her execution, the latter, Chapyuys, particularly sickened by the venerable lady's treatment. He wrote that as the King's Executioner had been sent north to deal with the rebels, Margaret had to be dispatched by a stand-in, 'a wretched and blundering youth who literally hacked her head and shoulders to pieces in the most pitiful manner.' Apocryphal accounts explain this as the result of Margaret point-blank refusing to lay her head down on the block and submit, declaring 'so should traitors do, and I am none!' Instead, she turned her head 'every which way,' instructing the executioner that, if he wanted her head, he should take it as he could. Chapuys concluded, in disgust, that 'there was no need or haste to bring so ignominious a death upon her' as due to her advanced age she would not 'in the ordinary course of nature live long.'

Across in Europe, Reginald Pole immediately declared himself the son of the martyr – and the Catholic Church apparently agreed, beatifying Margaret as a saint in the nineteenth century. Rather than the Princess Mary's husband, Reginald eventually became her Archbishop of Canterbury – the last Catholic Archbishop of Canterbury – during her reign and the Counter-Reformation. He died a mere twelve hours after her.

Margaret Tudor

Margaret Tudor (28 November 1489–18 October 1541) was the eldest daughter of Henry VII and Elizabeth of York, an elder sister to Henry VIII.

In her early teens she became Queen of Scotland; through her first marriage she was the grandmother of Mary, Queen of Scots, and through her second, that of Mary's second husband Lord Darnley – she is therefore twice-over the great-grandmother of James VI of Scotland/I of England.

Margaret was named for her paternal grandmother – the formidable Margaret Beaufort – and grew up alongside her surviving sister Mary and younger brother Henry in their mother's household in Eltham Palace. She had the typical Tudor auburn hair and dark eyes and had a talent for music, much like her mother and brother. From the tender age of six she was told to expect that one day she would cross the border and take her place as Queen of the Scots. Relations between Henry VII and James IV were tense, but eventually, in 1502, a peace treaty was agreed, and pretty Princess Margaret was the cherry on top. A marriage by proxy was undertaken in January 1503; Margaret was thirteen and James, thirty. Legend has it her little brother Henry – then of course just the Duke of York to his older brother Arthur's Prince of Wales – threw a tantrum when he was told that his sister, now officially Queen of Scotland, outranked him.

That summer, when the weather was more temperate, Margaret set off on her long progress north to the border at Berwick-upon-Tweed, where she was formally handed over to the Scottish court and proceeded on to Edinburgh. Although the union was of course one arranged for political rather than personal reasons, there seems to have been true affection between James and his child-bride. Margaret was homesick at first, as is to be expected, but soon settled in. She bore her first child at sixteen; she would bear six in total, although only the one son would survive to adulthood. James spoiled his queen and the Scottish court was pleasant and social; Margaret would probably have been happy.

In 1509, Henry VII had died and been succeeded by Henry VIII, who had no particular interest in upholding his late father's peace treaties. Henry declared war on France, putting James between a rock and a hard place, as he had a treaty with both sides. In the end, it was the 'Auld Alliance' that won out – France and Scotland were historic allies – and James moved against his brother-in-law.

Margaret was conflicted. She clung to her identity as a member of the English royal family, but held affection for her adopted homeland. She begged her husband not to go to war against her brother, claiming to have had prophetic dreams of his death and defeat. This was probably just rhetoric in an attempt to persuade her husband to abstain, but it turned out to be all too true; James met his death at the Battle of Flodden Field in September 1513, along with a devastating percentage of the Scottish nobility.

Margaret was widowed, the Dowager Queen, left quite literally holding the baby – the now James V was a mere seventeen months old. She would soon have another son, born after his father's death, but he was to die at just eighteen months. James IV had, in his will, appointed Margaret as regent during his son's minority, but only whilst she remained unmarried. Although Margaret's appointment as regent was confirmed by Parliament, it was done begrudgingly. Margaret was a woman, sister to an enemy king and known to hold anti-French sympathies. It was proposed that she be replaced by John Stewart, Duke of Albany, the closest male relative to the infant prince.

But it was agreed, even by her enemies, that Margaret was a more than competent leader. As such she held onto her position and within the year Scotland and France had agreed peace with Henry VIII. She may have been able to hold onto power – remaining de facto King of Scotland for the decade or more until the young James was considered ready to take over leadership of the country – but Margaret threw it all away (the men of the council sneered: typical woman!) for love.

Archibald Douglas, the Earl of Angus, had – upon his grandfather's death – taken up his place on the king's council. Upon their meeting, he and Margaret fell hopelessly in love and were secretly married only a few months later. Under the terms of her late husband's will, Margaret had now forfeited the right to be regent and guardian to her two young sons. The Duke of Albany became regent after all.

When the Duke arrived at Stirling to take possession of both the castle and the royal boys, Margaret initially resisted. Her brother Henry had been urging her to flee with her sons to England, but Margaret felt that to do so would be risking James's right to the throne. Eventually she realised it was futile and gave up her small sons to their new guardian.

By this time, Margaret was heavily pregnant by Douglas and the council allowed her to go into her female confinement in Linlithgow Palace, in southern Scotland. From there, the eight-months pregnant Margaret fled across the border back to England. Only weeks later, she gave birth to her daughter, Margaret Douglas, the future Countess of Lennox and mother of Henry Stuart, Lord Darnley. Douglas did not follow her, as to do so would have been forfeiting all of his Scottish lands and he appeared to love his position and income more than he now loved his wife. When Henry learned that his sister's husband had abandoned her, he sneered: 'Done like a Scot.'

Henry cared for his sister, lodging her in Scotland Yard, the ancient palace (or embassy, if you will!) of the Scottish kings in London. He and Cardinal Wolsey worked tirelessly to smooth things over with the Scottish council. After a year in exile, the dowager queen was allowed to return to her sons and husband in Scotland.

Whatever great love there had once been between Margaret and Douglas that encouraged her to give up everything, it was dead and gone now. Douglas had been living openly with his mistress whilst Margaret had been gone – most insultingly, on Margaret's money! Margaret removed herself from her husband's household and immediately began petitioning for a divorce. In 1518 she wrote to her brother:

> 'I am sore troubled with my Lord of Angus since my last coming into Scotland, and every day more and more, so that we have not been together this half year… I am so minded that, and I may by law of God and to my honour, to part with him, for I wit well he loves me not, as he shows me daily.'

Extremely ironically considering how his own marital history was to go, Henry was against the idea of divorce and would not countenance it. It seemed that poor Margaret was expected to lie in the bed that she had made, so to speak. However, her luck was on the turn. The Duke of Albany was in France, negotiating the marriage of James V to the French princess, and as a result she was allowed to resume her regency in his absence.

When the Duke returned to Scotland the pair became close, very close, close enough for some to say they were lovers. One nobleman wrote to Wolsey in England, saying that he believed the young James was going to be assassinated so that Albany would become king and marry Margaret. However, in hindsight it was probably just an association of convenience. When Albany returned to France in 1524, Margaret brought the now twelve-year-old James to Stirling and announced the regency was over as the young king had reached his majority. James declared his mother as his chief councillor.

Once again, Margaret was to let her heart rule her head and risk everything. She fell in love with Henry Stewart, a younger brother of Lord Avondale, and began to advance him. Douglas and his cronies were furious, doubly so when Margaret would not allow her estranged husband to attend council (as was his right as the Earl of Angus). Things escalated quickly, with Margaret even ordering cannons to be fired at him when Douglas arrived in Edinburgh with a crew of armed men.

Eventually, Margaret was persuaded to back down and allow Douglas back onto the council. It was the opportunity he had been waiting for; Douglas seized control and the young king. He was to remain in this position of power for the next three years. Margaret was incensed and her desire to be officially divorced and free of him became a real obsession. Over and over she begged her brother for his support and petitioned the Pope in writing. Finally, in 1527, the Pope granted the divorce and only a few months later Margaret married for the third time, to Henry Stewart.

Her brother Henry's reaction is very amusing, in hindsight. He wanted Margaret to disregard the Pope's divorce dispensation, declaring that marriage was 'divinely ordained' and protesting against the 'shameless sentence sent from Rome.' He probably thought it was extremely unfair that he couldn't get one of these 'shameless sentences' of divorce when he wanted one.

Not long after the marriage, James V managed to extricate himself from his erstwhile step-father's custody. Angus fled into exile in England. Now that she was free of Angus and her son was firmly on the throne, Margaret could turn her attentions back to what had originally been her foremost concern – improving relationships between England and Scotland. She attempted to arrange a meeting between her brother and her son, but although Henry was agreeable, James refused. Although he was fond and respectful of his mother, he hated the English with a passion, blaming them for both the death of his father and the continued patronage of the step-father who had held him in thrall for three years.

Margaret's life was on the downturn again. Her new husband was already cheating on her and burning through her money, just like Angus had before him. Their only child died in infancy and she soon began petitioning for another divorce. James refused her. She then began to write to her brother in England, requesting money, protection and even a place in his court. 'I am weary of Scotland', she confessed. At one point she even tried to run away across the border as she had as a younger woman, but James caught wind of the plan and immediately had her captured and brought back.

Margaret died of a stroke at the age of 52. The onslaught of her illness was rapid; so certain was she that she would recover that she never made a will. By the time anyone realised it was serious and sent for the king, it was too late; James arrived shortly after his mother had passed away.

Margaret was a Tudor to her bones, stubborn and passionate and larger than life, just like her famous brother. She too had scandalous divorces, defied tradition to marry where she pleased, hungered for power and wealth and proved herself an able ruler. Somehow, Margaret (and her sister, Mary) are often omitted, eclipsed by their nieces and grandchildren, the illustrious personages of Mary I, Elizabeth I, Mary, Queen of Scots, Lady Jane Grey – etc. In the television show *The Tudors* Margaret and Mary are even amalgamated into the same person!

When she wasn't preoccupied with her new beaus or desiring divorces, Margaret was steadfast in her wishes to see England and Scotland united in peace and friendship. It has a nice poetic justice, then, that through her great-grandson, the two countries were united under the same monarch and together, thrived.

Mary FitzRoy

Mary FitzRoy (1519–7 December 1557), was the only daughter-in-law of Henry VIII. A pawn for her noble family from the moment of her birth, she ended up holding all the cards when her brother and father found themselves on trial for treason.

Mary was born the daughter of the second most senior noble in the English peerage, and the granddaughter of the first. In 1529, her father, Thomas Howard, was given the care of Henry Fitzroy, the only acknowledged illegitimate child of King Henry. The Howards, as well as being high-ranking nobles, were kin to Henry's new love, Anne Boleyn, and it wasn't very long before this queen-in-waiting began to moot a marriage between little Fitzroy and Howard's daughter Mary. It seems that Anne Boleyn was rather fond of Mary Howard, who had been a member of her household and seemed to share many of her personal leanings, particularly when it came to matters of religious reform.

The teenagers were married in 1533 and Mary duly became the Duchess of Richmond and Somerset. Henry VIII was said to believe that the physical rigours of too much sex had hastened his elder brother Arthur's death – although, of course, it suited Henry to be known to think this, as he had been angling to get himself divorced from said brother's widow, Katherine of Aragon and kept being frustrated by the queen's protestations that her first marriage had never been consummated. Regardless of the motives behind Henry's order, Fitzroy had not been permitted to consummate his marriage with his Duchess, and so, when he died three years after their wedding, Mary was not permitted to keep any of the lands or income that should have been her due as a widow on the grounds that the marriage had not been a complete or official one.

Mary dipped into obscurity for a while, forced to sell her household items and jewels to pay her debts. She was still considered a catch;

in 1538 the king gave his permission for her to marry Thomas Seymour (the brother of Queen Jane) but, apparently, the headstrong Duchess resolutely refused. Her star rose again alongside her family when her cousin, Katherine Howard, was queen, and dipped again when she was executed after her adultery. Still, Mary remained at court, on the periphery of the royal family.

Her brother, the Earl of Surrey, suggested to Mary that she should seduce the king and become his mistress, or maybe even his sixth wife, if a marriage to her erstwhile father-in-law could be countenanced by the public. Mary was disgusted, and summarily informed her conniving brother that she would rather slit her own throat than 'consent to such villany'.

Surrey's scheming had started to go too far, and in 1546 he found himself on trial for treason. Surrey, a man of extreme self-importance, had decided to quarter the royal arms of Edward the Confessor, whom he considered himself descended from, into his own. Mary found herself deposing at her brother's trial, where she confessed both that her brother felt himself to have a right to the English throne, but also that he had prevailed upon her to seduce her father-in-law so that he might have more influence over the king through her. This was no more bluster and deviousness than most of the old English nobles, but Henry was aging, his son Edward a babe, and he was extremely sensitive to any perceived threat. Surrey was found guilty and executed. Henry tried to take his father, the Duke of Norfolk down with him too, but Mary did not testify against him, and in any event, Henry died before Norfolk's trial and so the old Duke was spared.

Mary never remarried, living out the rest of her life quietly on the fringes of her erstwhile in-law's courts, most likely having had more than enough of Tudor drama.

Grace O'Malley

Grace O'Malley or Gráinne Ní Mháille, (c.1530–c.1603) was Queen of Umaill, chieftain of the Ó Máille clan and a pirate (yes, a pirate) of Tudor Ireland. She is more commonly known by her nickname, Granuaile.

Granuaile was the only legitimate child of Eoghan Dubhdara Ó Máille – chieftain of the Ó Máille clan, based in Clew Bay, County Mayo. Eoghan (and therefore Granuaile) was a direct descendant of its founder and eponym, Maille mac Conall. Henry VIII was Lord of Ireland in name, but – for Granuaile's childhood at least – the Irish tribal princes were more or less left to their own devices. The Ó Máilles were a seafaring clan with a row of castles all along the coast at Clew Bay, facing out to the sea. They taxed all those who travelled through or fished in their waters. They were respected tradesmen and sailors, having merchant relationships with countries as far away as Eastern Europe.

It is unsurprising that Granuaile grew up with a strong love for the sea. As a child, she was desperate to be taken along with her father on his trading expeditions. Although her father was extremely relaxed with his daughter and inclined to allow it, her mother refused, on the grounds that ladies weren't allowed on ships, as their long hair would blow in the wind and tangle up in the ship's ropes. Undeterred, Granuaile sheared her hair off, earning herself the nickname 'Gráinne Mhaol' (from maol, meaning bald) which was eventually anglicised into Granuaile. Her indulgent father agreed to take her along on all his journeys from then on.

Once, returning from a trip to trade with Spain, the Ó Máille ships were attacked by the English. Granuaile was under strict standing instruction to hide below decks if they were ever attacked, but instead climbed up into the sail rigging, where she watched the battle for control of the ship from above. She noted that an Englishman was coming up to the rear of her father, who was engaged fighting another, and knew that the intent was to cut him down from behind. She scrambled nearer across the rigging and let herself drop down on top of the man, drawing her father's attention and saving his life. The Ó Máilles went on to defeat the English and return home safely.

Granuaile might have been an unusual girl, with an unusual skill-set and unusual freedoms, but there were some constraints of sixteenth century life she couldn't avoid. In 1546, she was married off to Dónal an Chogaidh Ó Flaithbheartaigh (Donal of the Battle), the tánaiste (or heir expectant) to the Ó Flaithbheartaigh (O'Flaherty) clan, meaning he would one day rule Iar Connacht, the area roughly equivalent to modern Connemara. Although not a love match, it was a fair one; the Ó Flaithbheartaigh clan were also seafarers, and their lands lay adjacent to that of the Ó Máille. The marriage resulted in three children; two sons, Owen and Murrough and a daughter, Maeve (or Margaret).

Dónal was reckless and war-hungry, always seeking fame and glory in battle. He once captured a fortress from the Joyce clan, earning said fortress the nickname 'Cock's Castle' due to his attitude and aggression. When Dónal was struck down and killed in battle, the Joyces immediately moved in and reclaimed their fortress. The newly widowed Granuaile took this as an affront and immediately moved to recapture it, doing so with more ease than her late husband had originally. The Joyces were so impressed with her that they renamed the fortress Caisleán na Circe, the 'Hen's Castle,' the name by which it is still known. It remained in Granuaile's family line until it fell into disuse. Legend has it that once, when Granuaile was an old lady, she took refuge at Hen's Castle from the English, who put her under siege there. Granuaile ordered that the lead from the roof be melted down and poured over the heads of the attackers. In the confusion that followed, a runner from the castle made it through the besieging forces and was able to summon help. The English were beaten back and Granuaile and her family freed.

As Dónal had never had the opportunity to be chieftain of their clan, the Ó Flaithbheartaighs did not honour custom and protect and provide for his widow. Granuaile took her children and a sizeable chunk of the Ó Flaithbheartaigh clan – who adored her – and returned to her Ó Máille homeland. With no husband or formal 'income', it isn't hard to see why Granuaile felt piracy was the best way to support herself and her people. As trade ships came through the Ó Máille waters, Granuaile's ships would stop them and demand either cash or a sizeable portion of the ships' cargo for safe passage the rest of the way. As she stopped other Irish ships as well as foreign traders (particular those from the rich trading colony at Galway Bay), this didn't particularly endear her to her fellow Irishmen. They appealed to Queen Elizabeth, as 'Lord of Ireland' to intervene. But the more involved and heavy-handed that the English became, the more Granuaile felt inclined to rebel. As well as carrying on her piracy, she began to aid those who were rebelling against Queen Elizabeth's overlordship, providing men, weapons and transport.

In 1566, Granuaile contracted another marriage, with one Risdeárd an Iarainn Bourke, called 'Iron Richard', an appropriate corruption of his Irish name as he is reputed to have always worn a coat of mail inherited from his Anglo-Norman ancestors. Like her first marriage it was politically astute; Richard had lands bordering her own (including the impressive and well-situated Rockfleet Castle) and was also being 'persecuted' by the English governors. The pair married under ancient Brehon Law (an ancient Irish civil code) for 'one year certain'. Granuaile spent most of that year on-board a ship, continuing her piratical ways, even giving birth to Richard's son Tibbot in the captain's cabin. The next day, her ship was boarded by Turkish pirates and Granuaile hefted herself out of childbed, grabbing her gun and heading straight into the fray. 'Take this from unconsecrated hands!' she is said to have shouted as she shot at the invaders.

As the year of marriage came to a close, Granuaile and her followers headed straight to Richard's Rockfleet Castle and locked themselves in. Richard and his men came to see what was afoot. Granuaile called out of a window, 'Richard Burke, I dismiss you,' effectively and legally ending the marriage under Brehon Law. The astute Granuaile however knew that her being in possession of the castle at the point of the 'divorce' meant it became legally her own. There were apparently no hard feelings between Richard and Granuaile – he remained loyal to her cause until his death, and in later life, Granuaile would refer to herself as 'Richard's widow' in correspondence with Queen Elizabeth.

Another interesting story is that of Granuaile at Howth Castle. Apparently, in 1576, Granuaile attempted to pay a courtesy visit to

Baron Howth. She was informed that the family was sitting down at dinner and she was refused access. Incensed at this poor hospitality, Granuaile abducted Baron Howth's grandson and heir and would not release him until a solemn promise was given that from that point onwards the Howth family would leave their gates open to visitors and set an extra place at every meal they sat down to. Lord Howth even gave Granuaile a ring as part of this pledge. The ring remains in the possession of Granuaile's descendants and at Howth Castle today, the agreement is still honoured by the Gaisford St. Lawrence family, descendants of the Baron Howth.

Meanwhile, Queen Elizabeth was extending the control over Ireland that her title afforded her. She appointed Sir Richard Bingham as Governor of the Irish territories, charging him to keep the peace. One of his first actions was to send guards to arrest Granuaile and have her hanged for her lifetime of crime. Contemporary records show that Granuaile, then in her mid-fifties, acted with dignity during what she believed would be the last days of her life. At the very last minute, her son-in-law offered himself as a hostage to the English. Granuaile was freed, on the proviso that if she ever returned to her rebellious ways, her daughter's husband would pay the forfeit with his life.

Things were at a stalemate for the next few years; Granuaile and her clan certainly did not give up their piracy, but it was never quite enough to be worth raising her wrath by retaliating. However, in 1593, all hell broke loose. Granuaile's eldest and most beloved son, Owen, was killed by the brother of Richard Bingham. On top of that, her youngest son with her first husband, Murrough, decided to join forces with the English. Heartbroken that he would do this after the murder of his own brother, Granuaile announced that Murrough was dead to her and never saw him again. Seizing the opportunity to once and for all finish Granuaile – who he called the 'nurse to all rebellions in the province for forty years' – Bingham captured her youngest son, Tibbot Burke and her illegitimate half-brother.

There was nothing for it; Granuaile decided her only hope was to appeal to Elizabeth directly, queen to queen. It is easy to understand how Queen Elizabeth's interest would have already been piqued; like her, Granuaile was an individual who had exceeded the limitations of womanhood and was showing great bravery in physically traveling to London to meet with her persecutor. Before agreeing to the meeting, Elizabeth sent Granuaile a 'questionnaire' of sorts, with eighteen questions, all about her life, her family, her 'career' and the finer points of Gaelic Law and the rights of women therein. Granuaile's argument was that all her piracy and rebellion was as a direct result of being denied her rightful inheritance from her first husband and that her legal right to rule her father's clan was questioned due to her gender, despite their overlord, Elizabeth herself, also being a woman. She also felt that Bingham had a personal vendetta against her family and needed to be curbed. Even further intrigued, Elizabeth agreed to meet with Granuaile, despite Bingham's loud protestations.

The unprecedented meeting took place at Greenwich. Granuaile had a dagger on her person, which was immediately removed from her. Granuaile swore that it was for her own protection and that she wished no harm to Elizabeth and so was allowed to proceed. At this point, however, she refused to bow, underlining that she did not recognise Elizabeth as Queen of Ireland. The atmosphere was extremely tense. According to legend, Granuaile had picked up a cold on her sea-crossing, and sneezed. A courtier offered her use of an expensive lace handkerchief to blow her nose with, but after Granuaile had so used the item, she tossed it into the fire. On-lookers were aghast at her rudeness. Elizabeth immediately scolded her for her extreme wastefulness. Granuaile replied that the Irish would not have kept and reused a handkerchief, even such a fine one as that, and so apparently they had higher standards of cleanliness than their English counterparts. The court held its breath, fully expectant that Elizabeth would immediately order that the rude Irish woman be executed. Elizabeth was silent for an uncomfortable moment before, thankfully, exploding into laughter.

Elizabeth proceeded to treat with Granuaile very fairly, expressing her respect for her both as a woman and as a leader of men. Three years older than Elizabeth herself, Granuaile had many freedoms that even Gloriana herself could only covet – the chance to lead her men into battle personally, to travel and explore the world, to take husbands and lovers at will and bear children. Elizabeth ordered that Granuaile's family members be set free and Granuaile herself be given respect and autonomy in her lands; in return, Granuaile promised to cease her support of the Irish rebels – and also to stop her piracy against English ships (all others were still fair game, apparently!). Richard Bingham was removed from his post as Governor of Ireland.

Finally, Elizabeth offered Granuaile the title of Countess; Granuaile respectfully refused, on the grounds that one queen cannot ennoble another. In 1627 however, Charles I made her son Tibbot Burke Viscount Mayo. Granuiale's descendants can be traced prominently through the nobility of both Ireland and Britain.

The peace between the two queens lasted for a little while, before Bingham was reinstated. Granuaile (probably quite bored at this point) went swiftly back to her old ways. She died in her mid-seventies, a fine old age, most likely at Rockfleet Castle, the fortification she had tricked from her second husband all those years ago. More than twenty years after her death, an English lord deputy of Ireland recalled her ability as a leader of fighting men, noting her continued fame and the respect for her that was still widespread among the Irish people.

Mary Grey

Mary Grey (c.1545–20 April 1578) was the youngest daughter of Henry Grey, Duke of Suffolk, and Frances Brandon, herself the daughter of Charles Brandon – great friend and confidante of Henry VIII – and Mary Tudor, his younger sister.

An unfortunate figure, Mary was described by an ambassador as 'little, crook-backed and very ugly' – it is probable that she had a more serious form of the scoliosis that we know plagued her ancestor Edward IV's brother, Richard III; she may have even been a dwarf! Nevertheless, through her royal maternal grandmother, Mary and her two sisters claimed the right to inherit the throne, a fact that would be constantly shaping Mary's life.

Mary was the third and final daughter of the family, following Jane and Katherine, who would both fall foul of their cousin monarchs. Jane, of course, is the better-known Grey sister – the 'Nine Days Queen' (although she actually reigned de facto for nineteen days). When Edward VI lay dying in the early summer of 1553, he balked at the idea of being succeeded by his fervently Catholic half-sister Mary, leaving a controversial will that superseded that of his father, Henry VIII. His throne was intended to skip the 'illegitimate' Tudor sisters, Mary and Elizabeth, plus an arbitrary handful of cousins (including Mary, Queen of Scots and Mary Grey's mother Frances Brandon) before settling on Jane. The Grey sisters were all young – at this time around the ages of 15, 12 and 9; most importantly for Edward and his advisors, they were Protestant.

As everyone knows, none of this went very well for 'Queen Jane'. The country rose up for Mary Tudor and Henry Grey, Jane and her husband Guildford Dudley were summarily executed in February 1554. Frances Brandon Grey and her two remaining daughters were in disgrace. Acutely aware of this, Frances took her Master of Horse for her second husband, efficiently signalling the end of her family's dynastic ambitions. This second husband inherited a lifetime stake in all of Frances's property after her death in 1559, so Katherine and Mary had very little to live on.

When Elizabeth came to the throne, she seemed to be sympathetic to her Grey cousins, appointing Mary as one of her Maids of Honour and granting her a royal pension. Katherine, the elder sister, was at one point seemingly being groomed as the childless Elizabeth's heir – there was even talk of a formal adoption and of marrying Katherine back into the Tudor bloodline on the Scottish side. Finally, life seemed to be going better for the unfortunate Mary Grey.

Unfortunately, Katherine fell unwisely in love and secretly married Edward Seymour, (nephew to Edward VI's mother Jane Seymour). She knew what she had done was imprudent – heirs to the throne were not permitted to marry without the express permission of the monarch – so she decided to keep the match a secret. Somehow, she managed to do this quite successfully until she was coming up to nine months pregnant. Terrified of the Queen's certain displeasure, Katherine went to Elizabeth's favourite, Robert Dudley (her brother-in-law through the marriage of Jane and Guildford). It didn't do any good. Elizabeth was enraged. Katherine and Edward Seymour were imprisoned in the Tower of London – in separate rooms (although this was obviously not strictly enforced, as Katherine managed to conceive and give birth to a second Seymour son during their imprisonment). Nevertheless, the marriage was annulled, said sons declared illegitimate, and eventually poor Katherine died of consumption at the age of only 28 – whilst still under house-arrest.

And so now there was only Mary Grey left in consideration – dependable Mary! Elizabeth was still quite fond of her, and surely she had learned from the mistakes of the rest of her family? Obviously not, because Mary too entered into a secret marriage in 1565. Mary waited for Elizabeth to leave court to attend the wedding of one of her Boleyn kinsmen before marrying the Queen's serjeant porter, Thomas Keyes, who was in charge of palace security. Mary apparently learned one lesson from her sister's fate – she ensured that there were a bevy of witnesses so that Elizabeth couldn't just declare that the marriage hadn't happened, as she had with Katherine.

Thomas Keyes was a bit of a bizarre choice, so much so in fact that some postulate that the timid Mary married him purely to rule herself out of the succession entirely – to remove herself from the game board, if you will. Keyes was a widower with a load of children, only a member of the minor gentry, as well as being twice Mary's age and height – apparently 6'8' tall! Sir William Cecil wrote that 'The Sergeant Porter, being the biggest gentleman of this court, has married secretly the Lady Mary Grey, the least of all the court... The offence is very great'.

Elizabeth was, predictably, unimpressed. She confined Mary to house arrest and Keyes to the Fleet Prison. The couple never saw one another again; Keyes was released from prison in 1569, but his health was irreparably affected and he died shortly afterwards. Before his death he asked Elizabeth if he could reclaim his wife and retire from court, but Elizabeth had refused. Afterwards, Mary petitioned the Queen for the right to adopt and raise her orphaned Keyes step-children, but Elizabeth wouldn't even allow her this. Eventually, however, after Mary had been under strict house arrest for over seven years, Elizabeth finally decreed she could be free to live where she pleased. Unfortunately, by now Mary had lost all of her friends and had far too little income to run her own household, so she ended up staying on with her erstwhile jailors, a rather unwelcome house guest! Eventually however, she did leave, 'with all her books and rubbish', as her warden ungraciously put it.

Mary seemed to be getting another chance. By the end of 1577 she had been rehabilitated to the extent that Elizabeth reappointed her as a Maid of Honour. Less than a year later however, the plague ripped through London, and Mary became ill. Having just enough time to write a will parcelling out her meagre belongings, she died on 20 April 1578, at the age of 33. Elizabeth granted her cousin an impressive funeral in Westminster Abbey, before allowing her to be interred there, inside her mother's tomb.

With Jane and Mary both dying childless, and Katherine's Seymour children considered illegitimate, Mary was the last member of a royal dynasty that never was, one where we may have had the Greys rather than the Stuarts. Fittingly, her portrait – painted during her imprisonment there in 1570 – hangs in the Prime Minister's country estate in Chequers, Buckinghamshire; in it, Mary proudly shows off her wedding ring and wears carnations to symbolise love, fidelity and remembrance – for her husband, no doubt, but also perhaps for her ill-fated sisters.

Penelope Rich

Penelope Rich, aka Penelope Blount, Countess of Devonshire (January 1563–7 July 1607) was a prominent English noblewoman during the reigns of Elizabeth I (her cousin) and James I. She was the sister of Elizabeth's 'toyboy favourite', Robert Devereux, Earl of Essex and scandalised her contemporaries with her extra-marital activities.

Penelope Devereux was born in Chartley Castle in Staffordshire, the eldest child of Walter Devereux, Viscount Hereford, (later also the Earl of Essex) and the unfairly infamous Lettice Knollys. Lettice was the daughter of Catherine Carey – the daughter of Mary Boleyn – making her Elizabeth's cousin through her mother, Anne.

Penelope was a star. Impressive pedigree aside, she was a beauty famed Europe-wide, with her golden hair and dark Boleyn eyes. The queen's miniaturist painted two miniatures of Penelope (when she was Lady Rich – in 1589 and 1590). One was given to James VI of Scotland (later James I of England), highlighting just how much of a sensation she must have been. She was accomplished, too – fluent in French, Italian and Spanish and a gifted dancer and singer; Penelope brought a youthful vigour to the court of her aging cousin Elizabeth.

Penelope's father died in September 1576; two years later, the widowed Lettice rather outrageously married the queen's lifelong favourite, Robert Dudley. This move not only earned Elizabeth's enmity, but pretty much scuppered the young Penelope's marriage prospects. It had been proposed for some time that Penelope would marry Dudley's nephew and heir Sir Philip Sidney, an impressive courtier slash poet (weren't they all!). After the marriage between Lettice and Dudley, the negotiations fizzled out.

So it was that the beautiful Penelope Devereux arrived unmarried at court in 1581, aged eighteen. Unsurprisingly, she was snapped up within a couple of months. Her guardian sought and obtained Queen Elizabeth's consent for Penelope to be married to the powerful Baron, Robert Rich, (later to become the Earl of Warwick). It is said that Penelope protested vehemently against the marriage, but her preference was ignored. She was duly wedded and became Lady Rich, providing her hated husband with a rather impressive seven healthy children.

Despite – or maybe because of – her unhappy domestic situation, Penelope continued to shine at court. Philip Sidney certainly seemed to have still held a torch for the wife he could have had; Penelope is usually taken to be the 'Stella' of Sidney's poetical magnum opus, the *Astrophel and Stella* sequence of sonnets. Interestingly, after Sidney died from battle wounds, Penelope's brother Robert (Elizabeth's new favourite after their stepfather Dudley's death in 1588) married Sidney's widow Frances Walsingham – the tangled families of Renaissance nobility!

Perhaps it was knowing just how beloved she was at court, perhaps it was trust in the powerful protection of her brother Robert, but by the mid-1590s Penelope had had enough of her unhappy lot. She was deeply in love with Charles Blount, Baron Mountjoy, a prominent nobleman. By 1595, their affair was an open secret. By 1597, she'd given birth to his son. Lord Rich seethed at the affront, but whilst his brother-in-law Robert Deveraux had the queen's love and favour, he dared not move against his scandalous wife.

In time, his patience paid off. Robert Deveraux was executed for treason in 1601 and Lord Rich lost no time in throwing his wife out of his house – along with her two small children by Mountjoy. Luckily, the relationship between the lovers was a strong one, and this was almost what they had been waiting for. Mountjoy brought Lady Rich to live formally with him, to all intents and purposes his wife. They soon had a third child together.

When James I ascended the throne, Mountjoy was created Earl of Devonshire. Despite their unusual marital arrangement, he and Penelope were well respected in the Jacobean court. Penelope was among the ladies who escorted James's bride – Anne of Denmark – when she entered London in 1603 and duly became one of her Ladies of the Bedchamber.

By 1605, Lord Rich had had quite enough of this ongoing humiliation and finally sued for divorce. Penelope cheerfully admitted publicly to her adultery, wanting nothing more than to be freed to marry her true love and legitimise their four children. The divorce was granted – however Penelope's request to remarry was not. But Penelope had been defying public opinion for years now, and she and Mountjoy married anyway, in front of their chaplain at home on Boxing Day 1605.

This complete flouting of canon law was too much even for the previously indulgent James, who banished the erstwhile favourites from court. Although it was obviously meant to be a mark of their disgrace, it was perhaps the happiest time in Penelope's rather tempestuous life. She was able to live quietly, a wife to her husband in all ways, mothering their young children. Sadly, there was to be no leisurely, loved-up 'retirement' for the Duke and Duchess of Devonshire. Mountjoy died just three months after their wedding. Penelope died the following summer, aged only 44, one of the last of the truly great ladies of the Tudor court.

Arbella Stuart

Arbella Stuart (1575–25 September 1615) was an Elizabethan and Jacobean noblewoman, considered by many of her contemporaries to be the rightful heir to Elizabeth I.

Arbella was the only child of Charles Stuart, 1st Earl of Lennox, (of the third creation), and Elizabeth Cavendish. Her father's mother was the daughter of Princess Margaret Tudor, elder sister of Henry VIII, making her a first cousin, twice removed, of Elizabeth I. Her father was the younger brother of Henry Stuart, Lord Darnley, second husband to Mary, Queen of Scots and thereby father to James VI of Scotland. She was – as one historian would put it – 'too royal for her own good'.

Arbella's father died when she was very young and at the age of seven she was orphaned completely and became the ward of her maternal grandmother Elizabeth Talbot, Countess of Shrewsbury; the indomitable woman who has come down to us through the ages as 'Bess of Hardwick'.

It is likely she had a fair amount of contact with Mary, Queen of Scots during her childhood, as Bess's husband, Lord Shrewsbury, was her jailer. Certainly, Mary willed Arbella some jewels and instructed her son James that he bestow upon Arbella the title 'Countess of Lennox', which was her right through her father.

Arbella received a thorough and excellent education. It is even speculated that the poet/playwright Christopher Marlowe was one of her tutors. She was formally educated well into her twenties, could speak fluent Latin, French, Spanish and Italian and play various instruments to a high standard. All of the household were instructed to refer to Arbella as 'Your Highness' and it seems that she was perhaps brought up with the expectation that she could one day be Queen of England.

There are contemporary reports that unfortunately Arbella was a difficult person to like. Apparently, she could be arrogant and haughty and this behaviour did not endear her to the courtiers and Elizabeth was forced to curtail her stays in court and send her back to Hardwick Hall on several occasions.

In the 1580s and '90s there was a general apathy towards James VI and Arbella was definitely considered one of the most natural candidates to succeed the aging queen. Arbella's name was incessantly bandied around Europe; there was marriage proposal after marriage proposal. The then pope even 'defrocked' his own cardinal brother in an attempt to have him marry Arbella and through her lay claim to the English crown.

Although there is evidence that Arbella periodically visited court and had correspondence with her cousin the queen, by and large she was kept secluded away in her grandmother's home, Hardwick Hall. Later, she would bemoan her upbringing as exceedingly lonely, and her home as a 'prison'. A few months before Elizabeth's death, rumour reached the queen's ears that Arbella was making plans to escape her grandmother's custody and had made an agreement of marriage with Edward Seymour. This branch of the Seymours were descended from Lady Catherine Grey, sister of Lady Jane Grey (the 'Nine Days Queen'), a granddaughter of Princess Mary Tudor, youngest sister to Henry VIII and Arbella's own great-grandmother, Princess Margaret Tudor. This proposed marriage would be uniting two families each with a relatively strong claim to the throne and absolutely could not be countenanced. Being a close relation of the monarch, it was illegal for Arbella to make any marriage whatsoever without express permission from the crown. When questioned, both Arbella and Seymour denied any intent to marry and the matter was dropped.

Elizabeth died in March 1603 and James VI of Scotland succeeded to the throne as James I of England. There were those who argued that James should have been excluded from the succession, due to his being foreign-born. Arbella, being his first cousin, was a junior branch of the same line, but importantly, *was* English-born and raised. Soon after the succession, malcontents contacted Arbella, attempting to embroil her in a plot to overthrow James in favour of herself. She refused, and immediately reported the conspiracy to the authorities. Despite her apparent disinterest in the throne, she was still considered quite a prize; in 1604, the King of Poland sent an ambassador to James asking for permission to make Arbella his queen. His request was denied.

Arbella's life actually improved under King James. She was considered First Lady of the Court and was close with James's queen,

Anne. It became clear however that James would never permit her to marry or have children who could ever go on to pose a threat to his own son and dynasty.

In June 1610, Arbella was in her mid-thirties and perhaps growing desperate for a last chance at happiness, at control of her own life. She entered into a secret marriage with William Seymour (also known as Lord Beauchamp), the younger brother of the Edward Seymour she had been linked with all those years ago. The two had been brought before James a year or so before to deny that they were intending to marry, so it appears that their relationship was long-standing.

It seems to have been a genuine love-match, for all that it seemed merely politically astute, and considering Beauchamp was a decade younger than his new bride. Once, when Beauchamp was taken ill with a cold, Arbella sent him a letter:

> 'I do assure you that nothing the State can do with me can trouble me so much as this news of your being ill doth; and, you see, when I am troubled I trouble you with too tedious kindness, for so I think you will account so long a letter, yourself not having written to me this good while to much as how you do. But, sweet sir, I speak not of this to trouble you with writing but when you please. Be well, and I shall account myself happy in being
>
> Your faithful, loving wife.
> ARB. S.'

The marriage was not discovered until the following summer. James was enraged at the deceit. The couple were imprisoned separately. Beauchamp – his presumption the greater, to marry one of the king's blood – was sent to the Tower, Arbella to be held at a private residence in Lambeth.

Their confinements, however, were not harsh and they lived in relative comfort. They were allowed to correspond and wrote many letters to one another, including the one quoted above. However, when James discovered that the pair were in communication, he resolved to send Arbella north to stricter circumstances, guarded by the Bishop of Durham. When Arbella was told of this she became distraught and hysterical. A doctor attended her on her journey north, but part-way there he reported to James that the lady was simply too ill to travel. Thus Arbella procured an important few months' delay.

Her correspondence with Beauchamp, it seems, had somehow continued and the two had concocted a plan. Somehow, Arbella persuaded an attendant to aid her in paying a last visit to her husband, whom she declared she must see before going to her distant prison. She promised to return. This credulous servant, led astray, perhaps, by sympathy for the star-crossed couple, not only consented to the request, but assisted the lady in assuming an elaborate disguise:

> 'She drew a pair of large French-fashioned hose or trousers over her petticoats, put on a man's doublet or coat, a peruke such as men wore, whose long locks covered her own ringlets, a black hat, a black coat, russet boots with red tops, and a rapier by her side. Thus accoutred, the Lady Arbella stole out with a gentleman about three o'clock in the afternoon. She had only proceeded a mile and a half when they stopped at a post-inn, where one of her confederates was waiting with horses; yet she was so sick and faint that the hostler who held her stirrup observed that the gentleman could hardly hold out to London.'

It is often noted that Imogen, the cross-dressing heroine of Shakespeare's *Cymbeline*, was inspired by Arbella.

Eventually, after a many-legged journey, Arbella made it to the harbour at Lee, where a French vessel was anchored waiting to take the lovers into exile where they could be free and together. But, alas, Beauchamp was not there. Arbella insisted that they wait for him, saying that she did not care to leave if it was not to be with her beloved husband. It was to prove a disastrous stand; the delay allowed the king's forces – by then informed of Arbella's disappearance – to apprehend her and take her to the Tower of London.

Heartbroken, Arbella finally gave in completely to the melancholic despair that had plagued her most of her life. Over the next four years of imprisonment she faded away; most reports claim she simply starved herself to death. She died on 25 September 1615 at the age of just 40. In the nineteenth century, during a search for the tomb of James I, her coffin was found in the vault of Mary, Queen of Scots, placed directly on top of that of the Scots' queen. Her sad ghost purportedly haunts the Queen's House at the Tower of London.

And what of her husband, William, Lord Beauchamp? He actually did escape the Tower that day. A cart had entered the enclosure to bring wood to his apartment. On its departure he just brazenly followed it through the gates, apparently completely unobserved. His servant stayed behind with orders to keep all visitors from the room, telling the warders that his master was in bed with toothache.

He made it to Lee but just missed Arbella, quite literally 'ships passing in the night'. Not knowing what to do, he boarded a ship to Flanders and escaped to the continent. After some years, and Arbella's death, James VI allowed him to return to England. He was to live through three successive reigns and prove himself a loyal man to the Stuart dynasty.

Sophia Dorothea of Brunswick

Sophia Dorothea of Brunswick (15 September 1666–13 November 1726) was Queen of England as the wife of George I, however never set foot in that kingdom; her husband had her imprisoned for over half of her life. Doomed by the tension and mutual hatred of her arranged political marriage, she was nevertheless remembered fondly by her children.

Sophia Dorothea was the only child of the Duke of Brunswick, but even this one lone daughter was much to the consternation of her wider family. Her father had promised his brother that he would not marry and produce an heir that may cause opposition to his dynastic ambitions (this brother was to become the Duke of Hanover). Sophia Dorothea's mother, therefore, was considered only the Duke's long-term mistress, which meant their daughter was legally illegitimate.

Despite these slightly hazy credentials, marriage proposals cropped up thick and fast for the engaging girl (she was at one point very close to becoming the future Queen of Denmark). At each turn, these marriages were blocked by the political machinations of the Duchess Sophia of Hanover, Sophia Dorothea's aunt by marriage, an imperious and haughty matriarch. Sophia of Hanover was also the heiress presumptive to the crown of England (being a granddaughter of James I) and was certainly no woman to be crossed.

Eventually, Sophia Dorothea's father grew enough in confidence to legally marry his mistress and legitimise his daughter. Duchess Sophia's response was to make it work for her by immediately recommending marriage between Sophia Dorothea and her own son and heir, George Louis. The teenaged Sophia Dorothea – who had been hankering after marriage with the handsome Duke of Wolfenbüttel – threw a tantrum when told of the change of plans. She hurled a miniature portrait of George Louis against the wall and shouted, 'I will not marry Pig Snout!' – an unflattering but rather deserved nickname her cousin was known by. Still, Duchess Sophia insisted, and despite her mother's protestations on her behalf, her father capitulated and the engagement was made. Distraught, Sophia Dorothea did absolutely everything she could to escape her impending marriage. There are reports that she fainted during her first meetings with both her future mother-in-law and her future husband.

The unlucky pair were married on 22 November 1682 and, unsurprisingly, the union was an unhappy one. The Duchess Sophia looked down on Sophia Dorothea for her 'base' birth and lingering taint of illegitimacy – as well as the stubborn behaviour she had shown when confronted with the marriage – and encouraged the wider family to treat her poorly. George frequently scolded and argued with her in public and, after the births of their son and their daughter, started to neglect her completely, shamefully trumpeting his mistress, Melusina von Schulenburg.

It was at this time that one of Sophia Dorothea's teenage paramours re-entered her unhappy life like your metaphorical ray of sunshine. Count Philip Christoph von Konigsmark – of Sweden – had made Sophia Dorothea's acquaintance when they were much younger, where they had flirted innocently; there is a lovely story of the two using their breath to steam up the glass of the palace windows and writing their names in the condensation. After years of close friendship, they began an affair in 1690, writing each other a series of passionate love letters. A handful of these went astray and were given over to Sophia Dorothea's father-in-law, who immediately sent Philip off to fight with the Hanoverian army against France in an attempt to staunch the scandal.

Exiled from Hanover in all but name – all other soldiers were given periodic leave to return, but he was not – Philip grew increasingly lovelorn for Sophia Dorothea. Eventually he deserted his post and rode for six days to return to Hanover – which only resulted in his exile being made official.

Meanwhile, George railed at his wife over her affair. Whilst circumspectly admitting nothing, Sophia Dorothea merely pointed out his own adulterous activities. Although their arguments had always been combustive, this one escalated to the point where George threw himself on his wife and began to strangle her, tearing out clumps of her hair for good measure. Her life was only saved because their aghast attendants finally came to their senses and pulled George away. Sophia Dorothea was nevertheless disgraced, and in the full and frightening knowledge that George would have his revenge on her sooner or later.

What happened to Sophia Dorothea next is shrouded in mystery. Sentenced to a form of house arrest, legend has it that Philip may have come back to spirit her away from Hanover and the fury of her husband. Whatever the truth of what happened, an attempted escape was futile and Philip disappears from the historical record without a trace – save a few deathbed confessions from palace guards who say they killed the troublesome Count on the orders of George and threw his body into the River Leine…

Announcing himself as 'divorced' due to his wife's adultery was not enough for George, and he had Sophia Dorothea imprisoned at the Castle of Ahlden and forbidden to see her children ever again. She remained at Ahlden for 33 years, until her death of liver failure on 13 November 1726. She had spent the long decades incessantly petitioning to see her children but was never allowed. Apocryphal stories tell of a young George II desperately trying to breach Ahlden Castle to reach his mother, even going so far as attempting to swim the moat, but all in vain.

Just before her end – from what she then knew to be her deathbed – Sophia Dorothea wrote a letter to George, denouncing him for his incessant cruelty to her and cursing him from beyond the grave. George refused to allow mourning in Hanover or England and was furious when he heard that his daughter's Prussian court was wearing black in honour of their Queen's mother. Sophia Dorothea's body was left in a casket in Ahlden's cellar, ostensibly forgotten, whilst those who had cared about her waited for her husband's attention to slide. In May 1727 she was quietly moved to Celle, her childhood home, and buried beside her parents under cover of darkness.

Caroline of Ansbach

Caroline of Ansbach (1 March 1683–20 November 1737), once the 'most agreeable princess in Germany', was Queen of Great Britain, famous for her lively mind and canny grasp of politics.

The princess of a tiny German state, the young Wilhelmina Charlotte Caroline was orphaned and raised by her godparents in the liberal and enlightened court of Prussia, where she was exposed to ideas and education that would have once been beyond her wildest dreams. An impressive scholar, Caroline blossomed into a much sought-after bride. She was also highly principled; she turned down the hand of the Archduke Charles of Austria, also heir to the throne of Spain and one day to become the Holy Roman Emperor, because she could not in good conscience covert from Lutheranism to Catholicism. Even after a lifetime of learning, Caroline would always bear the hallmarks of a late start with education; her handwriting was atrocious and she was unable to spell many simple words, even the names of her closest friends. Her husband once teased her that she wrote 'like a cat'.

In 1705, the nephew of the Prussian Queen Sophia Charlotte, who had been Caroline's beloved guardian, visited the Ansbach court incognito, wanting to inspect the young woman he had heard so much about. This was the young Prince George Augustus of Hanover, and he liked what he saw. His father had been unhappy in his own marriage and was therefore minded to grant his heir a little more freedom to follow his heart. 'I found that all I had heard about your charms did not nearly equal what I saw,' George wrote to her dazedly after his visit. Luckily, Caroline too had been impressed by her 'mysterious suitor' and travelled to the Electorate of Hanover to be married to its heir later that year. Their son and heir, Frederick, shortly followed.

It was perhaps an omen of the fraught relationship that was to develop between Caroline and her oldest child that she was separated from her newborn almost immediately. A few months after the birth, Caroline contracted smallpox and was quarantined. Smallpox was the disease that had killed her father and step-father, but Caroline overcame it, only to be struck down with pneumonia. She was kept isolated and away from the vulnerable baby prince, but her husband George stayed by her side, even falling ill himself. Their marriage was a very loving one. George kept blatant mistresses (as society all but expected of their royal men), but Caroline was the very epitome of other-cheek turning, remaining gracious, faithful, silent on the topic and even keeping her husband's mistresses in favour in her own household.

When her father-in-law succeeded to the throne of England in 1714, George and Caroline sailed for their new realm, which Caroline would never again leave. Prince Frederick stayed behind in Hanover, being brought up by his tutors rather than his parents. Caroline was invested as the first Princess of Wales for over two hundred years, the last one having been Katherine of Aragon. As George I was formally estranged from his wife, there was no Queen-Consort, and so Princess Caroline was the highest-ranking woman in the country. A secondary court sprang up around her, with intellectuals, composers, philosophers and scientists, as well as writers and artists hastening to the drawing room of this impressive, enlightened princess. Isaac Newton even performed experiments on light refraction for her entertainment.

When Caroline came into contact with the concept of inoculation, she was intrigued. It was a very new idea, and most people thought it was insane to purposefully inject your loved ones with a disease. Caroline ordered that experiments be undertaken – first asking prisoners who had been sentenced to death if they wished to instead receive the vaccination. When the convicts all survived, Caroline had the experiment repeated again with orphaned children, before – now convinced of its effectiveness – having some of her own children immunised. Caroline then flaunted these healthy children in the centre of society, in her attempt to impress upon everyone that inoculation was straightforward, safe, and was, indeed, to be encouraged. These actions helped to popularise and propagate the idea of vaccination, saving countless lives.

Although Caroline's life in England seemed like it could have been a happy one, she found herself collateral damage in the ongoing tensions between her husband, George Augustus, and his father the king. After a clash between the two men over her second son's christening, Caroline found herself under house arrest, banished from court, and forbidden to see any of her children, including this newly-born prince (who sadly only survived a few weeks of life). Caroline was stricken, even daring to visit her children in secret.

The power struggles between her husband and father-in-law came to an end in 1727 with the death of the latter in June of that year; come October, Caroline was crowned Queen-Consort alongside the new George II. But the family strife wasn't at an end. The couple's eldest son Frederick was summoned from Hanover in 1728 and immediately began to clash with his parents. The now adult prince was a gambler and a philanderer and seemed to make a point of opposing his parents at every turn, personal and political. It was partly due to this tension – but mostly due to Caroline's extraordinary capabilities – that she, rather than the Prince of Wales, was left as Regent when George II was out of the country. Indeed, the whole kingdom knew that their portly, precocious queen completely outshone her husband. A popular satirical poem of the time joked:

> 'You may strut, dapper George, but 'twill all be in vain,
> We know 'tis Queen Caroline, not you, that reign.
> You govern no more than Don Philip of Spain.
> Then if you would have us fall down and adore you,
> Lock up your fat spouse, as your dad did before you.'

As queen, Caroline continued in the German model of the enlightened princess. She surrounded herself with collections of books, art and curiosities (she famously had two 'unicorn horns') as well as planning numerous beautiful gardens that still exist, in part, today. She even allowed the palace gardens to be opened to the public when the royal family were away. She preoccupied herself with good works, including pressing for penal reform, and the support of unwed mothers, as well as continuing to nurture philosophy, culture and the sciences. The famous French writer Voltaire was impressed, writing:

> 'I must say, that despite all her titles and crowns, this princess was born to encourage the arts and the well-being

> of mankind; even on the throne she is a benevolent philosopher; and she has never lost an opportunity to learn or to manifest her generosity.'

It was in her celebrated library in St James Palace where the end started for this indomitable queen. Always famously plump (one visitor to court wrote of her 'bosom of exemplary magnitude'), Caroline had become so overweight and riddled with gout that she had to be wheeled around in a decorative wheelchair that had begun life as a prop in a court masque, and in 1737 she collapsed while perusing her books. Her final pregnancy in 1724 had left her with an umbilical hernia and now a loop of her intestines was protruding from the hole. If her doctors had known to just push it back in, Caroline may have survived, but instead they cut it off and destroyed her digestive system, leaving her dying in agony for over a week.

Even on her deathbed, Caroline's gregarious personality and winning ways shone through; she joked and bantered with her surgeon and told him to imagine he was slicing up his hated wife rather than his queen, and when an ill-placed candle set fire to one of his assistant's wigs she laughed so hard that they had to pause the procedure while she composed herself.

Caroline finally succumbed on 20 November, George holding her hand. At the end she had tried to make him promise he would marry again, but he refused. When she was gone, the king was thrown into paroxysms of grief, declaring that he had never seen another woman who was 'worthy to buckle [Caroline's] shoe' and ordering a pair of matching coffins with removable sides, so they could lie together once more when he died, which in the event was 23 years later.

Maria Fitzherbert

Maria Fitzherbert *née* **Smythe**, previously **Weld** (26 July 1756–27 March 1837) isn't particularly at home in a collective of royal wives, but nor is she truly a mistress; she was the secret, illegal wife of the future George IV.

Maria was born to a respectable, Catholic family. Attractive and clever – she was educated in Paris – she made an excellent match at eighteen when she was married off to a wealthy landowner, Edward Weld, the holder of Lulworth Castle in Dorset. The now Maria Weld was set to be just another of the scores of women now invisible to history, but her life changed course when – only three months after the wedding – Weld was killed falling from his horse. So sudden was this death that he hadn't yet updated his will to take his new bride into account, and so Maria was returned to her family, widowed and penniless. Three years later Maria married again, but this husband – Thomas Fitzherbert – was killed during an anti-Catholic riot in 1781. At least, this time there was an annuity for her, as well as a London town house.

It was from this position that the twice-over widow entered London society. Maria, still in her mid-twenties, was a rare beauty. In 1784, the *Morning Herald* proclaimed excitedly:

> 'A new Constellation has lately made an appearance in the fashionable hemisphere that engages the attention of those whose hearts are susceptible to the power of beauty. The widow of the late Mr Fitzherbert has in her train half our young nobility. As the Lady has not, as yet, discovered a partiality for any of her admirers, they are all animated with hopes of success.'

At the head of this pack of susceptible admirers was the crown prince himself. Prince George was younger than Maria – only 21 – but already the very archetypical playboy 'big spender'. As the story goes, the prince caught sight of the comely widow one night at the opera and fell instantly in love. But Maria was no fool, nor did her strict religious morals permit her to entertain the idea of becoming anyone's mistress – even the prince. Undeterred, Prince George swore to Maria that he would marry her, if that's what it took – he'd do whatever he needed to do to make her his.

Maria probably felt exasperated, but safe. Both George's age and the Royal Marriages Act precluded him from marrying without his father's and parliament's permission, which surely would not be forthcoming for a Catholic twice-over widow of common descent – by royal standards of the time, Maria could hardly be *worse*. But George was not a man who was used to hearing no, and it wasn't long before he resorted to rather drastic measures. On the evening of 8 July 1784 Maria was very alarmed to receive the prince's surgeon, who informed the widow (with, one hopes, a good poker face) that the heir to the throne had stabbed himself in the chest and swore he would tear his bandages off and bleed to death if Maria did not immediately come to his side. What could Maria do, but assent?

Maria was joined at the prince's bedside by her friend Georgiana, Duchess of Devonshire, whose own account of the evening states:

> 'We went there & she promis'd to marry him… but she conceives as well as myself that promises obtain'd in such a manner are entirely void.'

However, in the moment, Georgiana had even taken a jewel from her own finger for the couple to use as a betrothal ring.

As safe as Maria felt, shielded by the Royal Marriages Act, she still fled abroad literally the very next day. George did not take the hint, writing to her incessantly for the next year and a half until eventually Maria was worn down, and agreed to marry him. George paid off a chaplain to commit the high treason that was marrying the heir to the throne without the king's consent, and thus the two were wed in December 1785.

So, did the shine wear off for George once he was able to eat his cake? Well – yes and no. George and Maria lived quite contentedly together for over a decade, living a rather merry life in Brighton. But George never did learn to budget and his debts racked higher and higher. Eventually the situation was so dire that he had to go cap-in-hand to Parliament and ask for a bail out. They pressed their advantage – they'd arrange for George's allowance to be increased, but only if he married a nice Protestant princess of their choosing and got busy with the heir-making. George had no choice but to agree.

In June 1794, Maria received a letter informing her that their 'marriage' was over as he was preparing to marry his first cousin, the appropriately Protestant Caroline of Brunswick. Quite what Maria thought of this turn of events we will never know, but George seemed to think he'd handled it gracefully, informing his brother that the parting was amicable. He continued to pay her allowance and encouraged his friends to continue respecting and hosting her in the same manner as they had before.

Parliament-approved Caroline of Brunswick might have been, but she was not Prince-approved. The story goes that George was revolted upon first sight of his new bride. 'I am not well. Pray get me a glass of brandy,' he swooned in revulsion (Caroline wasn't massively impressed with him either, for what it's worth).

George spent his entire wedding day in a drunken stupor (and apparently spent his wedding night passed out in an open grate). Apparently, moments before the ceremony was to begin, George murmured to his brother, the Duke of Clarence (the future William IV), 'tell Mrs. Fitzherbert she is the only woman I shall ever love.' Rather surprisingly, however, Caroline fell pregnant almost immediately and nine months later gave birth to George's only child, the Princess Charlotte Augusta. That same week George updated his will, bequeathing all his 'worldly property… to my Maria Fitzherbert, my wife, the wife of my heart and soul', adding that although she 'could not avail herself publicly of that name, still such she is in the eyes of Heaven, was, is, and ever will be such in mine…'

George formally separated from Caroline, paying her off to leave the country, and distracting himself with his favourite pastimes of mistresses, spending, and spending on mistresses. Meanwhile, Maria lived a quiet life, weathering George's flip-flopping attitude towards her; sometimes he sought a reunion, sometimes he ranted to people about how they had had no marriage, and that *she* had bullied *him* into the sham ceremony all those years before.

Whatever George's public stance on his relationship with Mrs Fitzherbert, his private position is made evident through some of his final acts. On his deathbed in 1830, the now King George IV placed Maria's 'get well soon' letter under his pillow and requested that when it was all over that he be buried with a miniature of Maria around his neck. His wish was granted. It was quickly discovered that George had kept all of his letters from Maria, dating all the way back almost fifty years, charting their rather unconventional love story. The letters were, of course, destroyed. George's younger brother, now William IV, met with Maria, and reviewed the documents she kept in her possession that apparently proved the existence of her marriage to his brother beyond any legal doubt (the Royal Marriages Act notwithstanding). William accepted the truth of the matter and offered his sister-in-law the title of Duchess, which she politely refused. She asked only the permission to wear widow's weeds and to dress her household servants in royal livery. William readily agreed to these requests, and so Maria saw out her remaining seven years of life more officially a royal widow than she had ever been seen as a royal wife.

Princess Charlotte

Princess Charlotte (7 January 1796–6 November 1817) was the only child of George, Prince of Wales (later to become King George IV) and Caroline of Brunswick. Had she outlived her father and her grandfather, King George III, she would have become Queen of the United Kingdom, but she died suddenly following childbirth at the age of 21. Without this untimely death, it's likely that Queen Victoria would never have been born at all.

In 1794, the Prime Minister – William Pitt the Younger – decided that something must be done about the unpopular Prince of Wales (a figure famously lambasted in *Blackadder the Third*: 'We hail Prince George, we hail Prince George!' 'No, it's "we hate Prince George, we hate Prince George"…'). George had to be persuaded to marry and beget heirs to the throne. The feckless prince had already attempted marriage – to his long-term and wholly unsuitable mistress, Maria Fitzherbert. Their 'marriage' was promptly invalidated as they hadn't sought (and wouldn't have received!) the monarch's permission to marry as required by the Royal Marriages Act, 1772. George kept Maria Fitzherbert on as a mistress, of course, along with several other doting women. He had absolutely no interest in making a marriage for the good of his family – but William Pitt knew his weak spot…

Despite his generous income, Prince George was in dire financial straits; by 1794, his princely salaries weren't even enough to cover the interest on his mountain of debt. Parliament promised George a 'pay rise' if he would marry and get busy making royal babies; a reluctant George agreed. His shortlist consisted of two German princesses, both of whom were his first cousins – one from his father's family and one from his mother's. Most people favoured the latter – Princess Louise of Mecklenburg-Strelitz, who by all accounts was virtuous and beautiful, as was appropriate for a future queen. However, Prince George's then-favourite mistress – Lady Jersey – decided to promote the interests of the other princess, Caroline of Brunswick, who she thought would be less of a rival for George's royal affections. So, despite the fact that Caroline was rumoured to be rather unappealing and had a bit of a scandalous reputation, George chose her as his bride – sight unseen – and dispatched a diplomat to fetch her to Britain.

It was a dire mistake. Caroline was brought to meet her future husband at St James' Palace. Prince George took one look at her, and cried out, 'Harris, I am not well, pray get me a glass of brandy.' But Caroline got her own zinger in, remarking, 'I think he is very fat and nothing like as handsome as his portrait!' Needless to say, it wasn't a match made in heaven. George turned up to the wedding ceremony drunk off his face, having sent his brother (the future William IV) to Maria Fitzherbert with a sweet but pointless declaration of his true love. The royal couple did the baby-making deed three times and then separated. One day short of nine months after the wedding day, Caroline gave birth to a daughter, christened Charlotte Augusta after both of her grandmothers. Although at this point the royal family were hated for their excess and tendency towards madness, the little princess was taken to British hearts, her birth widely celebrated. Prince George wrote to his mother, advising her that his wife had given birth to: 'an immense girl, and I assure you notwithstanding we might have wished for a boy, I receive her with all the affection possible'.

Almost immediately after Charlotte's birth, Prince George drew up a will, the prime purpose of which seemed to be insulting his wife. In it he left all his worldly goods to Maria Fitzherbert and dictated that Princess Caroline would have nothing whatsoever to do with the raising of their daughter. In fact, Caroline was only allowed to see her infant once a day and only in the presence of her nurse and her governess. Characteristically not giving a fig what her estranged husband wanted, whenever she could Caroline took baby Charlotte on carriage rides through the streets of London, to universal approval and applause from the crowds.

Charlotte grew up being used as a pawn and a point of contention between her warring parents. She had a lonely childhood, living in a household of her own, her only company people who were paid to be with her. Eventually, her governess's grandson – three years Charlotte's junior – was brought to her household to be her playmate.

Forty years later that boy – then the Earl of Albemarle – would recall these years in his memoirs. In them, Charlotte is remembered as a tearaway, a tomboy who loved to be outside and cause mischief. In one particularly charming tale, Albemarle remembers a crowd gathering hoping to see the young princess. The two children immediately slipped outside of the house and – totally unrecognised – joined the crowd.

By 1805, it was clear that Charlotte would one day sit on the throne. George and Caroline were never to be reconciled, which means that there would be no legitimate son to come before Charlotte in the line of succession. King George took control of his heir's education. Charlotte was popular at court – contemporaries thought her warm and engaging with a candid, informal manner. Of course there were some that thought a princess should be more dignified – and Charlotte was often told off for wearing dresses that showed off her ankles – racy! Charlotte was an excellent pianist and horsewoman and enjoyed listening to Mozart and reading Jane Austen novels, although her spelling, grammar and handwriting were apparently atrocious.

In 1811, King George descended into his 'madness' for the final time, and Prince George was sworn in as Regent. He immediately cracked down on his 15-year-old daughter, not allowing her to do anything or go anywhere and decreeing that she always be chaperoned. The bored and rebellious Charlotte immediately engaged in a string of infatuations with any young man she had any contact with – usually cousins. These harmless little affairs were supported by the rest of the royal family turning a blind eye, as they disapproved of the straits that the Regent was keeping his daughter in.

By 1813, the Napoleonic Wars were finally going well for Britain and George took the opportunity to consider his daughter's marriage – a difficult question indeed, for whoever married Charlotte would become King of Great Britain as Charlotte's consort. The Regent favoured William, Hereditary Prince of Orange, son and heir-apparent of Prince William VI of Orange. Unfortunately, Charlotte did not, as the first time she met him he was drunk and disorderly.

Meanwhile, at a party at the Pulteney Hotel in London, Charlotte met a Lieutenant-General in the Russian cavalry, Prince Leopold of Saxe-Coburg-Saalfeld. The impoverished prince called on the princess at her invitation, remaining for three quarters of an hour. Scandalous!

Afterwards he wrote to the Prince Regent apologising for any perceived indiscretion. George was impressed with the lad but did not by any stretch of the imagination consider him as a possible suitor for his daughter. He continued to press the Orange marriage.

Charlotte had no choice but to play for time. She tentatively agreed to the marriage negotiations and stalled by throwing things she believed the Prince of Orange and his council would not agree to into the negotiations. She demanded she never be forced to leave Britain. They agreed. She demanded that Britain be inherited by their eldest son, the Netherlands by their second. They agreed. Finally, Charlotte demanded that her mother be always welcome in their house. Princess Caroline was famously outspoken against the marriage with the Prince of Orange; unsurprisingly, here he disagreed, and Charlotte had the excuse she wanted to reject his proposal.

Prince George was livid. He sent word that Charlotte was to be kept 'under house arrest' in her household and see nobody until she was taken out of London to Windsor. When told of this, a panicked Charlotte raced out into the street, desperate to avoid falling into the control of her father and the marriage that she didn't agree with. A neighbour, seeing her distress from his window, helped the inexperienced princess hail a hackney cab which she asked to take her to her mother's house. Charlotte and Caroline immediately summoned a selection of sympathetic Whig politicians to advise them. Most of the royal family also gathered, including her uncle, Frederick, Duke of York, who had a warrant in his pocket to secure Charlotte's return to her household (and her father) by force if it proved necessary. After lengthy arguments, the Whigs advised her to return to her father's house; she unwillingly did so the following day.

Charlotte's panicked flight through the streets of London was a hot topic of conversation. The general public adored the princess and the press clamoured that she should be at liberty to leave her father's household and marry who she chose – she was, after all, over eighteen. Despite the best efforts of the populace, the press and even some members of the royal family, Charlotte's isolation continued. In 1814, it was heightened when her mother left Britain for an 'extended visit' in Europe (Charlotte was never to see her mother again).

By 1815, Charlotte had grown quite used to her quiet life. All the men – suitable and otherwise – she had harboured infatuations for eventually married elsewhere. Charlotte had kept up a correspondence with the impoverished Prince Leopold she had met some years before and began to grow a genuine affection for him. She began to relentlessly petition her father for the right to marry him. The Prince Regent, however, had not given up all hope for the marriage with the Prince of Orange. Charlotte soon put him straight on that front; 'No arguments, no threats,' she wrote, 'shall ever bend me to marry this detested Dutchman.' In the face of overwhelming support for his popular daughter, George gave in.

Unfortunately, Leopold was otherwise occupied fighting Napoleon on the continent. It wasn't until late February 1816 that he arrived in Britain and immediately went to Brighton to be interviewed by his potential father-in-law. Charlotte had dinner with the two, and afterwards gushed:

> 'I find him charming, and go to bed happier than I have ever done yet in my life … I am certainly a very fortunate creature, & have to bless God. A Princess never, I believe, set out in life (or married) with such prospects of happiness, real domestic ones like other people.'

Unbelievably the Prince Regent too found himself rather a fan of Leo, telling his daughter that he 'had every qualification to make a woman happy'; quite an endorsement!

On 14 March, the engagement was announced in the House of Commons, to great public and political acclaim. The people were happy that their beloved princess was being allowed to make a love-match; the politicians were just pleased that the drama of Charlotte's teenaged rebellion looked likely at an end.

Charlotte and Leopold married on 2 May 1816. On the wedding day, huge crowds filled London, causing traffic problems to the extent that the bride and groom were late arriving at the venue! Leopold dressed for the first time as a British general; Charlotte's wedding dress cost over £10,000. The pair gazed at one another fondly throughout the ceremony, smiling broadly, and the mischievous Charlotte was heard to giggle when the impoverished Leopold promised to with all his worldly goods endow her.

After a few months honeymooning and getting to know one another properly, Charlotte and Leopold returned to London for the summer, where they were the darlings of society, greeted with raucous applause wherever they went. When it was reported that Charlotte had been taken ill at the opera, the public clamoured for news until it had to be publicly announced that Charlotte had suffered a miscarriage, but was recovering. Despite this early setback, Charlotte and Leopold's marriage thrived. They were a perfectly matched pair of opposites, what with Charlotte's exuberance and Leopold's calm attitude. When Charlotte became too excited, Leopold would say only, 'Doucement, chérie' ('Gently, my love'). Charlotte teasingly began calling her husband 'Doucement'. By the end of April 1817, it was announced that Charlotte was pregnant again, and this time it seemed she would carry the baby to term.

Charlotte purposefully did little during her pregnancy; having been prescribed a strict diet and occasional blood-letting – standard and accepted obstetric practice at the time. Although her due date had been 19 October, her contractions did not start until the evening of November 3rd. Her doctor, Sir Richard Croft, sent for the officials whose task it was to witness the birth of the next in line to the throne. However, 3 November became 5 November and still there was no sign of the royal baby. Charlotte – understandably – was in dreadful discomfort and weak from the strain and the fact that they hadn't let her eat since her first contraction.

At 9pm, Charlotte finally expelled a large, stillborn boy. All efforts were made to resuscitate the little prince, who was noted to resemble the royal family in his features, but he had clearly been dead for some while. An exhausted Charlotte took the news numbly, mumbling that it was obviously 'God's will'. Leopold, who had been present at his wife's bedside throughout the protracted labour, was devastated; he took an opiate and retired to his bed. Despite her gruelling fifty-hour labour and devastating loss, Charlotte seemed to be relatively well. She was given some wine to drink after her long fast and noted it left her feeling rather tipsy.

At midnight, Charlotte began to complain of pains in her stomach. She then began to vomit, have trouble breathing and started to bleed. Alarmed, Sir Richard Croft started the then-accepted treatment for postpartum haemorrhaging and called for Leopold to be roused and brought back to the bedside. Dr Stockmar, Leopold's own physician tried and failed the first time to wake the prince, deep in his opiate sleep as he was, before returning distraught to the princess. By this point Charlotte was insensible and raving. Stockmar left the room to try his luck with the comatose prince once again, but Charlotte called him back, voice urgent. By the time he made it back to the bedside, Charlotte was dead.

The country plunged into deepest mourning. One journalist remembered it 'as though every household throughout Great Britain had lost a favourite child'. Merchants ran out of black cloth with even the poor and homeless tying armbands of black on their clothes to mark their respect. The mourning was so complete that the makers of ribbons and other fancy goods (which could not be worn during the period of formal mourning) petitioned the government to shorten the period, fearing they would otherwise go bankrupt. Shops closed for two weeks, as did the Royal Exchange, the Law Courts, and the docks; even gambling dens and brothels shut down on the day of her funeral.

Perhaps surprisingly, most devastated of all were Charlotte's parents. The Prince Regent was described as prostrated with grief and quite unable to function. He couldn't even bring himself to attend the funeral. Princess Caroline, sojourning on the continent still, learnt the news of her daughter's death as passing gossip and fainted in shock and grief. Upon recovering, she cried out, 'England, that great country, has lost everything in losing my ever beloved daughter.' Even the jilted Prince of Orange burst into tears at hearing the news, and his wife ordered the ladies of her court into mourning out of respect for her husband's feelings and the general tragedy of having lost someone so beloved and so young.

Leopold was never to recover from this great loss. He wrote to Sir Thomas Lawrence:

> 'Two generations gone. Gone in a moment! I have felt for myself, but I have also felt for the Prince Regent. My Charlotte is gone from the country—it has lost her. She was a good, she was an admirable woman. None could know my Charlotte as I did know her! It was my study, my duty, to know her character, but it was my delight!'

Leopold would go on to become the first King of the Belgians, after Belgium gained its independence from the Netherlands. He was one of the most favoured and trusted advisers of his niece, the future Queen Victoria, and in 1840 arranged a marriage between her and his nephew, Prince Albert of Saxe-Coburg and Gotha.

Charlotte was buried in St. George's Chapel, Windsor Castle, on 19 November 1817. Her baby son was placed at her feet. Their tomb's monument was paid for by public donation. Charlotte's tragic death did much to raise awareness of childbed death, and led to significant changes in obstetric practice, with obstetricians who favoured intervention in protracted labour, including in particular the more liberal use of forceps, gaining ground over those who did not. Although Sir Richard Croft was never formally blamed for the princess's death, three months later he committed suicide, wracked with guilt.

The death of Charlotte and her baby caused a succession crisis. She had been the only legitimate grandchild of King George. The press began to panic, pressuring George's brood of unmarried, 40-and-50-something sons to get busy. The King's fourth son, Prince Edward, Duke of Kent and Strathearn, had always been far removed from the pressures of the court. He lived in Brussels with a mistress, who he dumped so quickly her head probably spun. Edward unceremoniously proposed to Leopold's sister Victoria, Dowager Princess of Leiningen and did his duty. Their daughter, Princess Alexandrina Victoria of Kent, would be crowned Queen Victoria of the United Kingdom in 1837.

I do hope these little tales have whetted your appetite to know more about these wonderful women, to peek behind the curtains of romance and legend that so often drape them, and which – in the interests of narrative – I've often had to repeat here. Please do get in touch with me on social media if you'd like to chat about these – or any – forgotten royal women, or if you'd like any fiction or non-fiction book recommendations. Let's try and keep these ladies in the light.